Inspired Kitchens

for Modern Living

Our showroom is bursting with fresh ideas for your home

SOLUTIONS
BATHROOM & KITCHEN CENTRE

121 Mansfield Road, Sutton-in-Ashfield, Nottinghamshire NG17 4FL

01623 515793

Open: Mon - Fri 9am - 5.30pm. Sat 9am - 5.00pm. Sun 11am - 4.00pm

Welcome to

taste
derbyshire & nottinghamshire

Welcome to taste
issue 5 – with a new twist…

Welcome to taste Derbyshire and
Nottinghamshire. This is the fifth edition
of our book championing all that's best
in food and drink in our area.
Derbyshire and Nottinghamshire are
counties blessed with probably the
greatest number of food and drink
outlets in the Midlands, producing
everything from speciality puddings,
honey, smoked meats, farm-reared
meats, cheese and herbs, to locally
brewed beers. In this edition we are
featuring clients new and old, those
with established businesses of many
years and those new on the block.

Our recipe section is brimming with
ideas for you to try, all of them
home-cooked and home-tasted! The
signature dishes are from chefs around
the counties; these are some of their
favourites and their know-how really
shines through as they put together
some culinary delights.

Our thanks to Denby Pottery for the use
of their cookware. We also feature their
history and their latest designs.

To all those who have contributed to this
edition, be they advertisers or writers,
we would like to say a hearty thank you.

We hope that you all enjoy this latest
edition of taste.

Jane Plant,
Editor.

what's inside

Stories of food and drink from around our counties **pages 6 – 61**

Fantastic recipes for you to try including signature dishes from local chefs
pages 62 – 132

Places to buy The Ingredients
pages 144 – 155

The Inspiration *Restaurants to try*
pages 156 – 165

The Environment *Kitchens to work in*
pages 166 – 169

taste

Meet th

supplie

e

rs....

'There's always room for a pudding' says Angie

Despite what we say after our main course – "I just couldn't eat another thing!" – given a few minutes we are ready for pudding. I am in favour of puddings ('sweets' are too posh for me), hence I am a big fan of the puddings lovingly created by Angie Cooper at The Pudding Room, especially her apple pies.

As proprietor of The Pudding Room since 2001, Angie has created a much envied business. In her new purpose-built premises near the historic market town of Ashbourne, she makes beautiful meringues, pies, gateaux and all sorts of sensuous desserts, most of which are bought by the catering trade to serve to their dining clientele. Angie Cooper has a slogan, 'because there's always room for a pudding', and how true this is. Most of us (although not me) would sacrifice our starter to enjoy a delicious dessert.

The art of making a good dessert demands patience, and cold hands when making pastry. Blending mouth-watering concoctions and displaying them in an appetising manner is the way great cooks like Michel Roux and James Martin have led the field for many years. Angie Cooper has achieved this level of skill.

The Pudding Room is a member of both The Peak District Food Group and East Midlands Fine Foods. They use as many local ingredients as possible in their cakes and puddings to optimise the finished product. Some suppliers used at the moment are Peak District Dairy at Tideswell (milk and cream), Derbyshire Mushrooms at Atlow near Ashbourne, Heage Windmill for some flours and Field House Foods at Horsley near Derby (herbs and so on).

Many of the products in the range are developed from traditional recipes perfected over many years.

Angie Cooper's skill in creating her mouth-watering desserts has been acquired over many years of practice; if you would like to try any of her desserts she can be found at most farmers' markets. Go on – there's always room for a pudding! GP

Farmers' Markets where you can buy Angie's products

1st Saturday of the month; Wirksworth, Memorial Hall/Gardens.
2nd Saturday of the month; Belper Farmers' Market, in the Market Place, Belper.
Last Saturday of the month; Bakewell Farmers' Market, at the Agricultural Centre, Bakewell.

Shows Angie will be standing at in 2009

JUNE
Derbyshire County Show: Sun 28th 2009.
Elvaston Castle Country Park, Elvaston, Derbyshire
www.derbyshirecountyshow.org

AUGUST
Ashover Show: Wed 12th 2009. The Show Ground, Ashover, Derbyshire S45 0AU
The Ashbourne Show: Sat 15th 2009. The Polo Ground, Osmaston, Ashbourne, Derbyshire
www.ashbourneshow.co.uk

SEPTEMBER
Chatsworth Country Fair: Fri 4th, Sat 5th & Sun 6th 2009. Chatsworth Estate, Derbyshire.
www.chatsworth.org
Hayfield Country Show & Sheepdog Trials: Sat 19th & Sun 20th 2009. Hayfield, High Peak SK22

The Pudding Room, Ashbourne
Telephone 01629 540413. 07866415030
www.thepuddingroomderbyshire.co.uk

Peak District Dairy
Where Quality Comes Naturally

Peak District Dairy is in the heart of the Peak District National Park.

They specialise in delivering the finest quality dairy products to their valued customers and are able to adapt to their changing needs. They supply their own milk, cream and free-range eggs and make their own range of salted and unsalted butter, ice cream and farmhouse yoghurts. Their cows are grazed on the limestone grassland above Tideswell in Derbyshire at 1,100 feet above sea level.

They also supply a broad and diverse range of quality products and items like spring water, bread, fruit juice and a full range of English and Continental cheeses. They are agents for Longley Farm, Coombe Castle, Fage UK, The National Forest Spring Water and New English Teas.

Their ice cream is available in lots of delicious flavours and a wide variety of pot sizes including 120ml (with spoon in lid), 500ml, 1 litre, 5 litre (napoli) and 10 litre catering packs. Different flavours are made on request, so if you fancy something different, contact them. Their ice cream vans and trailers are on sites around the Peak District National Park. They are also available for special events and shows. Contact Robert on 01298 871786 or mobile 07867 533965 for more information.

The new Farm Shop/Café/Ice Cream Parlour is NOW OPEN

Peak District Dairy's new Farm Shop/Café/Ice Cream Parlour is now open in the centre of Tideswell village, where you will be able to try their award-winning products. They also have a full range of quality English and Continental cheeses. You can see an impressive selection of the best locally produced foods including Cocoadance chocolates, Irene's jams and marmalades, Field House Foods herbs and oils, Ibbottson's of Ashford pickled onions, Crips oven baked wheat and potato chips, The National Forest Spring Water, Taste of the Moorlands biscuits and cakes, Foxhill Foods pasta and curry sauces and Brookfield Bakery freshly baked bread and cakes daily.

The café seating area is upstairs where you can take time to relax and enjoy a light snack from the varied menu of freshly prepared foods, or just have a drink of tea or coffee or even a real fruit smoothie or a milkshake made with their real dairy ice cream. Maybe you just want to relax and enjoy a cake or an ice cream sundae made with a selection of their twelve flavours of the day. All the time you can sit and watch their widescreen picture frame that plays photos of their products, awards, local scenes and pictures from the past. If time is of the essence you can take one of their many 'snacks to go', including hot and cold sandwiches, soup, pies, cakes or even an ice cream of your favourite flavour, not to mention the many hot and cold drinks to go.

Peak District Dairy supplies direct to the retail and catering trade in their fleet of temperature-controlled vehicles and to milkmen/women for the doorstep trade. Peak District Dairy's aim is to provide you with the best quality dairy products available. At Peak District Dairy, quality comes naturally.

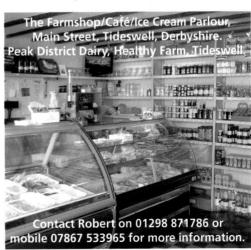

The Farmshop/Café/Ice Cream Parlour, Main Street, Tideswell, Derbyshire. Peak District Dairy, Healthy Farm, Tideswell.

Contact Robert on 01298 871786 or mobile 07867 533965 for more information.

Collect 'Gold' in Chatsworth!

Peak Ales are now selling their products from their brewery premises at Cunnery Barn on the Baslow to Chatsworth Road, and I went to get some! So, a trip into the countryside for you could be rewarded with a nice drop of Chatsworth Gold, Bakewell Best Bitter or Noggin Filler, a winter ale that has proven really popular.

'Having a good idea in business is only the first step in the long road to success,' owner Robert Evans was quick to explain. 'You have to ensure that at all stages quality remains to the fore and that your product, in our case bottled and cask beer, hits the mark every time in terms of consistency and that we maintain high standards in customer service.'

Setting up your own company is, to say the least, a risky business and you don't get many chances to get it right. Setting their sights on a place in the Peak District, Robert and David Smith, his brewing consultant, had a chance conversation with the landlord at the Devonshire Arms, Beeley and the rest, as they say, is history! Their brewery, set in lovely old barns in the delightful Chatsworth Park, provides an idyllic setting for a run out and a top up supply of beer!

Awards have come thick and fast for Peak Ales, who have risen to prominence in the brewing industry since 2003. Noggin Filler won "best bottled beer 2007" and Bakewell Best won "best cask ale 2006" – both of these awards came through the Beer Hunter at the Derby Evening Telegraph, which they were pleased with because they're local awards. Chatsworth Gold won "best beer in the speciality beers category" at the Doncaster Beer Festival 2008.

The production of bottled beers, which includes

Bakewell Best, was the next project and these are now on sale through the Farmers' Market Shop in Bakewell, the Chatsworth Farm Shop in Pilsley and Ibbotson's of Ashford. In addition they are signed up with the Direct Delivery scheme run by The Society for Independent Brewers and Enterprise Inns. This will enable them to be found in more of Derbyshire's pubs!

Increased production has led to further investment by Peak Ales. Stainless steel casks, a rare commodity to get hold of, have been purchased to meet the growing consumer demands. Stuart Wragg, who joined the business in 2006, has been an extremely valuable addition to the team and he was joined by Michael Robinson in September 2008. He has quickly settled into the brewing team and his contributions have added greatly to the company's efficiency.

The Beers

Bakewell Best Bitter
Bakewell Best Bitter is a robust amber-coloured ale. It is dry and firmly bitter, with some roasted malt flavours and plenty of grassy hops.
Alcohol by volume – 4.2%
Great with – crisps, savoury snacks and bold, strong flavours like stew or a ploughman's Cheddar.

Swift Nick
A traditional English session bitter, with a fruit and hop aroma. There are balanced flavours of

malt and hops leading to a dry bitter finish.
Alcohol by volume – 3.8%
Great with – crisps, savoury snacks and all manner
of mild to medium flavoured dishes such as pastas
and salads.

Noggin Filler
A classic traditional dark winter ale. Maris Otter
Pale Ale, Crystal Malts and roast barley combine
with Fuggles hops to create this distinctive and
warming beer, ideal for the winter months.
Alcohol by volume – 5.0%
Great with – mince pies and turkey.

DPA
A higher gravity pale ale. DPA is a distinctive and
refreshing beer that is well hopped with Goldings
for a smooth and slightly sweeter taste with a hint
of spice.
Alcohol by volume – 4.6%
Great with – crisps, savoury snacks, a rack of lamb,
a ploughman's or chicken.

Chatsworth Gold
A golden beer made with honey from the
Chatsworth estate. The delicate sweetness is well
balanced with the bitterness from Goldings and
Fuggles hops.
Alcohol by volume – 4.6%
Great with – crisps, savoury snacks and all manner
of delicious locally produced menus!

Peak Ales, Barn Brewery, Cunnery Barn,
Chatsworth, Bakewell DE45 1EX
Tel: 01246 583 737

Robert Evans

"He brews it, I use it…"
says Debra Evans of Peak Ales.

Flemish beef and beer stew

3 slices smoked bacon – diced
4 large onions, cooked, halved crosswise
and cut into 1/2 inch wedges
2 tsps. brown sugar
1 tbsp. cider vinegar
1 tbsp. vegetable oil
2 lbs. boneless beef for stew, cut into 1
inch cubes and patted dry
3 tbsps. all-purpose flour
3/4 pint Peak Ales Bakewell Best Bitter
1/2 tsp. dried thyme

Recipe
Cook bacon for about 5 minutes in a
flameproof casserole over medium heat,
turning occasionally, until crisp. Transfer
bacon to paper towels with a slotted
spoon and set aside.

Add onions to drippings in pan and cook
for about 20 minutes over medium low
heat, until very soft. Sprinkle with brown
sugar, increase heat to medium high and
cook for about 8 minutes, stirring often,
until onions are rich golden brown. Add
vinegar and season with salt and pepper
to taste. Transfer to a bowl.

Preheat oven to temperature 350°F, 180°C
or gas mark 4. Heat oil in casserole.

Add meat in batches and cook for 6 – 8
minutes per batch, turning occasionally,
until meat is browned on all sides.
Sprinkle with flour and stir well. Cook for
1 minute, stirring constantly.

Add Bakewell Best Bitter, thyme, onions
and bacon and remove from heat.

Cover casserole and transfer to oven.
Bake for 1 to 1-$\frac{1}{2}$ hours, or until meat is
tender.

Recipe from Peak Ales,
Barn Brewery, Cunnery Barn,
Chatsworth, Bakewell
DE45 1EX Tel: 01246 583 737

Colston Bassett Store

A hidden gem in one of the most picturesque villages in Nottinghamshire

Steeped in history, Colston Bassett's original village store was taken on by Jan and Martin Lindsay 5 years ago when they transformed it into a haven for food lovers. The Store is simply a delight with bread, freshly baked in the village taking pride of place in the inglenook and jams and chutneys displayed on a dresser topped with reclaimed oak. The off-license is housed in the old sitting room complete with Victorian fireplace and greeting cards take up one of the walls in the red and black tiled hallway.

The delicatessen counter offers over 40 cheeses from the British territorials through to the small artisan producers of goats and ewes milk cheese. Customers are encouraged to try new things and there are always cheeses on taste at the weekend. The charcuterie section includes the very best Parma and Serrano hams, salamis, wild boar proscuitto and several English cured hams whilst olives and antipasti are great 'ready to go' food hard to resist on a summer's evening with a chilled glass of wine.

"We are very keen on the provenance of our food but we don't buy local for the sake of it" said Martin "You couldn't get more local than the Stilton down the road or the fabulous Sparkenhoe Red Leceister and Lincolnshire Poacher, but when it comes to other products we'll go for the best and work closely with Brindisa for Spanish foods and Vallebona for Italian. Neals Yard and the Fine Cheese Co. are hard to beat if you want cheeses in mint condition."

As with all products sold, the Lindsays have insisted on top quality: Vera's eggs from the next village scoop up all the prizes at the poultry shows, Lubcloud Dairy deliver organic milk and cream, and Redhill Farm in Lincolnshire will make sure you don"t miss out on your weekend cooked breakfast with their free range bacon and sausages.

One of the most popular events at Colston Bassett Store are the Wine Tasting Evenings and customers will find an extensive selection of over 80 wines in the off license ...anything from Cloudy Bay (when we can get it!) to amazingly good value Berrys House Red. Alongside there is a good range of unusual beers from local and UK brews to Continental and Eastern ales.

In 2007, the fully licensed Garden Café Restaurant was added. The day starts off with daily baked scones and cakes served with Union Natural Spirit coffee moving into lunchtime with quiches, tomato tarts, ploughmans and continental platters using produce from the deli and salads of smoked chicken or Cornish crab. Desserts are tempting with toffee pavlovas and lemon meringue pie being especially popular and tea is served out of retro stainless steel covered teapots into muted pastel teacups.

In 2006, Colston Bassett Store was voted "the best village shop in the East Midlands" by a top team of foodies, including Heston Blumenthal, Henrietta Green and Nick Nairn. The shop was given the accolade in the BMW 1 Series Good Food Ride book which highlights the best places to eat, shop and visit in the UK if you're a foodie fan.

Customers will also find stylish displays of homewares, gifts and jewellery as well as a Vintage section with fabulous skin handbags and Art Deco pieces. A great selection of greeting cards and wrapping paper means the customer need look no further!

With the Garden Café and our non food sections of the shop, Colston Bassett Store could be the One Stop Destination for you. Come and be tempted !

GARDEN CAFÉ
RESTAURANT
AT COLSTON BASSETT STORE

Open everyday except Monday

Store tel: 01949 81321
Café tel: 01949 823717
info@colstonbassettstore.com
www.colstonbassettstore.com

denstone hall
FARM SHOP & CAFÉ

Denstone Hall Farm Shop and Café has already won a number of richly deserved awards and developed a loyal clientele since opening in July 2007. Beautifully situated on the Staffordshire/ Derbyshire border between Uttoxeter and Ashbourne in the village of Denstone, the family run business is located in the old milking parlour which has been lovingly restored, creating a successful mix of old and new.

The shop itself has a lovely welcoming atmosphere and displays a stunning range of local and seasonal produce. There it sells a fantastic selection of local and own grown free range beef, lamb, pork and chicken.

They also have an extensive deli counter supporting local cheese producers and sell some fabulous award winning Huntsman pie's. Don't miss out on is their award winning speciality pork and brambly apple sausages. Delicious!

The cafe has just been awarded Staffordshire Tea Room, 2008, where all food is freshly produced on site. Some of the current favourites are Leek and Potato soup, Welsh Rarebit with beer mustard and Fish Pie. The Courgette Cake and Apple and Plum Crumble have also developed a legendary reputation. Sunday lunches are proving to be very popular so be sure to call and make a booking.

For more information visit
www.denstonehall.co.uk or call: 01889 590050

Bob Pitchfork originally worked as a chef, but he spent his childhood on a farm where the year's harvest had to be preserved without modern methods such as freezers!

Bob started serving traditional pickles with modern food, which proved to be a winning combination, whilst working in a restaurant. The traditional pickles he created won awards.

Mr Pitchfork Pickles can be bought direct or at one of the local shops or farm shops they supply. All the chutneys, pickles and jams are hand-made with quality ingredients and treated with a good pinch of TLC!
For more information contact Bob Pitchfork : W39 Nottingham Business Centre, Lenton Boulevard, Nottingham NG72BY
07761 428961 or 01159 178037
email: robert.pitchfork@ntlworld.com

The best of local food at
Chatsworth farm

Specialising in the best of local and regional food, Chatsworth farm shop offers quality produce fresh from the estate, tenant farms, Derbyshire suppliers and small food producers.

Chatsworth farm shop won Farm Retailer of the Year 2009 in the National Farmers' Retail & Markets Association awards. The shop has a simple philosophy – it aims to source primarily from the estate, secondly from the estate's tenant farmers, thirdly from Derbyshire producers and then from other quality suppliers within the UK wherever possible.

Traditional butchers on the award–winning butchery will guide you through the vast array of meat, poultry and game. Delicious home-cooked meats and pies are available from the delicatessen counter, and their bakery provides wonderful fresh bread and cakes.

The food

Chatsworth farm shop is lucky to have a wealth of talented producers within easy reach of the farm shop, and prefers to source from small local suppliers wherever possible. Over 60% of the farm shop income is generated from produce from the Chatsworth estate.

The animals

Animal welfare is very important at Chatsworth, and they breed and rear contented and healthy livestock. They know that good husbandry towards their animals, which are reared and prepared nearby, will mean that they taste better too.

The family of suppliers

Good food begins with their suppliers. The skill and knowledge of their trusted

shop

Farm shop manager André Birkett

producers shines through in the food. Great care and attention goes into the food they produce, and they know most of the producers they buy from personally – some have been supplying them for as long as thirty years.

The family of staff

Chatsworth farm shop has a team of experts on hand, from butchers and bakers to talented chefs – all are happy to answer questions and to advise you. You can see them at work as you go through the farm shop.

The restaurant

Offering fresh home-cooked food in a beautiful space, the farm shop restaurant is the perfect place to unwind after a busy shop.

The chefs create delicious seasonal recipes using as much local produce from the farm shop as possible. Most of the food served in

the restaurant can also be purchased from the farm shop.

The history

Established by the Duchess of Devonshire in 1977, the shop sold beef and lamb from the estate farms, and venison from the park. Its aim was to sell Chatsworth's produce direct to the people who wanted to eat top quality, locally grown food. Since then the farm shop has developed and diversified, growing from strength to strength to become an acknowledged leader in its field.

Chatsworth farm shop,
Pilsley, Bakewell, Derbyshire DE45 1UF
www.chatsworth.org

Stichelton

maturing well for its age

When an opportunity to visit a farm arises, I never miss it, especially when it involves food production, and even better when it is cheese. Cheese has been on our menu for thousands of years. Ancient records show that sheep herding was very prominent in the Middle East. Current records show that Welbeck has developed Stichelton, the first organic raw milk blue cheese produced in Britain since the late 1960s.

Joe Schneider proudly shows of his cheese.

Before the cheese, let me explain a little about the Welbeck Farm Shop. Opened in 2007, it is on the Welbeck Estate just south of Worksop and boasts an array of food, much of it locally produced and sourced, from fresh organic vegetables to ready-made meals. The shop has an open and friendly feel and is notably very spacious. I was greeted by Farm Shop Manager Michael Boyle, who was raised on the estate and was instrumental in the opening of the shop three years ago. I immediately felt at home as Michael showed me around and introduced me to each department. Everywhere I went staff were beavering away, either making fresh pies or preparing soup for the restaurant, but by now I was eager to get to the cheese. This necessitated a drive to the Creamery on Collingthwaite Farm.

On the way Michael took a slight detour around the Welbeck Estate to give me a flavour of where the produce for the shop comes from. Having never visited the Welbeck Estate before I was astounded to see its extent (17,000 acres!) and also the array of beautiful properties built hundreds of years ago, standing majestically against a misty and snowy backdrop.

Once at the Creamery the words 'Food Miles' were immediately dispelled as I was shown a stainless steel pipe that runs from the herd of Holstein Friesian cows to the Creamery across a gap of about twenty feet. So it's a case of food yards here! At the dairy I met Joe Schneider, who, along with Randolph Hodgson (Neal's Yard Dairy), is the

mastermind behind Stichelton. Their goal is to create a cheese that has echoes of the past, with creamy, gentle flavours, long since abandoned due to the rule that Stilton must be made from pasteurised milk.

Joe explained that it would have been 'tempting to build a purpose-built dairy', but in the interests of tradition it was decided to convert the 250-year-old barns on Collingthwaite Farm. What a wise decision. It has atmosphere, and a feel of the past that a new building would never give. Obviously renovation was a little more costly, but well worth it even if only to see the original

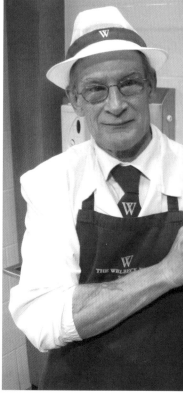

floorboards! Donning the obligatory blue coat, hat and shoes followed by a hand wash, we descended into the Creamery where Joe's next job, cutting the curd, was about to begin. Stichelton cheese is made from unpasteurised milk, a small amount of rennet and an even smaller amount of starter, making acidification low. Is it Stilton, you ask? Well, it's made from the same recipe but with unpasteurised milk. It also scores with the fact that Stilton can only be made in Nottinghamshire, Leicestershire and Derbyshire. However, it gets a little more complicated because Stilton has a PDO (Protected Designation of Origin) that stipulates it can only be made from pasteurised milk.

A new name needed to be found. So Stichelton, a name that Joe tells me was the original name for Stilton, was born. I loved watching Joe cut the curd, and was even more in a dream when we went into the

drying rooms and the delicate aroma of maturing cheese wafted around. Joe proceeded to produce differing ages of cheese to taste. It was fascinating to see just how much of a difference there was in cheeses that were only three or four weeks apart in age. All I needed now was a glass of port! Stichelton isn't pressed; the cheese sits in hoops in a warm room for five days and is then 'rubbed' using kitchen knives. Then it is placed in the drying rooms, where after six weeks it is pierced to allow the blue veining to form. Six weeks later it is ready for sale.

Forty tons are produced each year with potential for more. I for one hope that Joe doesn't go into mass production, as his current daily involvement is vital to keeping Stichelton unique and consistent in its quality.

My tour was completed when Michael

presented me with a big wedge of Stichelton – what a way to finish the day.

Why not visit Welbeck Farm Shop and see for yourself what is on offer? Their produce includes the freshest of locally grown fruit and vegetables, home reared and prepared meats, as well as a wide range of additional produce. Whilst there, pick up some Stichelton – you won't be disappointed. Or, if you visit the fashionable Covent Garden area of London, you can pick some up from co-creator Randolph Hodgson at Neal's Yard Dairy.

My thanks to Michael and Joe for their time and for making my day most enjoyable.

www.thewelbeckfarmshop.co.uk
Welbeck, Worksop
Nottinghamshire S80 3LW

Croots Farm Shop

With beautiful views over the rolling green expanses of the Ecclesbourne Valley, what more idyllic place could you imagine to do your family shopping?

The increased emphasis on a healthy lifestyle and healthy food makes us all conscious about caring for our environment, and the suffocating squeeze of the big supermarkets makes us recoil as they try to streamline us all into the same mould.

Croots Farm Shop is set conveniently on Wirksworth Road, just off the A6 in Duffield and yet among the green fields of a seventy-acre farm.

Steve Croot, co-owner of Croots Farm Shop, has been a passionate grower of fresh herbs, salads and vegetables all his life. From small beginnings growing herbs in his back garden in Huddersfield, Steve soon found uses for all the different herbs he grew and hit on the idea of producing herb-flavoured oils and vinegars. Demand grew, and Steve started producing commercially and moved his business to his father-in-law's farm at Duffield. The rest, as they say, is history!

Meeting and talking to Steve about the farm shop is an experience in itself, as his passion for supplying quality food to his customers is quite an obsession. He is constantly searching the local market place for fresh produce to stock. Let's take you on a tour of the premises.

The store is airy and welcoming, with pale wicker baskets setting the tone for your shop. The produce on offer has been sourced locally within a fifty-mile radius wherever possible, using suppliers with high commitment to quality ingredients.

The butchery department is a main feature and meat is cut, trimmed and prepared on the premises. Homemade sausages are a speciality and local beef, pork, lamb and chicken can also be bought ready-marinated in exotic sauces. The deli counter offers top quality cheeses from around the counties, many of which are hand-made in small quantities.

Fresh seasonal fruit and vegetables come from south Derbyshire, with a keen emphasis on delivering them from the grower as soon as possible after picking. From Tideswell, Peak District Dairies supply fresh milk, butter and cream, as well as a variety of award-winning ice creams.

A variety of speciality breads are delivered daily from Luke Evans' bakery at Riddings, and to accompany your cheeses, Mr Pitchfork's Pickles from Nottinghamshire are made with ale, apple, caramelised onion, and many more varieties to choose from.

Field House Foods produce their own range of infused oils, vinegars and herbs, which are produced on site. Fruit preserves come from the kitchens of Irene Norris in Youlgreave, and Derbyshire bees produce local honey for The Real Honey Apiary at Somercotes.

& Kitchen

You may serve yourself from the large freezers filled with frozen vegetables and berries. You can also find pain au chocolate, pain au raisin and butter croissants, to prove overnight and then bake in your own oven in just 8–10 minutes, fresh for breakfast. For a healthy take on crisps, Crips produce oven-baked potato crisps with a selection of flavours.

The Ashbourne area supplies buttery shortcake biscuits with additions such as rosehip and blackcurrant or honey and almond. Croots Kitchen produces homemade scones and cakes which are just as lovely as ones you'd bake yourself. You can also buy the famous Derbyshire Oatcakes, which are delivered to the shop fresh from the producer. There is also a range of local beers from the likes of Nutbrook Brewery at West Hallam, Amber Ales from Pentrich and The Derventio Brewery at Ashbourne.

And to recapture bygone days, the Bon Bon Company provide a colourful, eye-catching display of old-fashioned sweets. To complete the relaxing shopping experience, the coffee shop serves breakfasts until 11am and light lunches until 2.30pm using ingredients from the farm shop.

When you have finished your shopping, you can sit and have a coffee and watch the young Shire horse foals sleeping in the field at the front, giving you a chance to reflect on how different this is to the hustle and bustle of fighting your way through the supermarket crush, rushing to try and read the labels to buy good quality food. Here at Croots the work has been done for you, and the peace of the surrounding countryside echoes the feeling that not only is your shopping bag full of wholesome food, but also you have done your bit to take care of our own environment here in Derbyshire.

CROOTS
FARM SHOP & KITCHEN

Farnah House Farm Wirksworth Road, Duffield DE56 4AQ
www.croots.co.uk

Shop opening hours are: Tues – Sat 9.00 to 5.00, Sundays & Bank Holidays 10.00 – 4.00, Mondays – CLOSED. The coffee shop closes at 4.30 pm Tue – Sat and 4.00 pm on Sundays

Holloway Village Butchers

Robin Maycock Butchers in Holloway, Derbyshire is famous for its farm-fresh, locally sourced meat, all produced in Derbyshire and prepared in their own licensed premises at the rear of the shop.

The shop was established in 1850 by Thomas Walker and traded in the Walker family name until 1977, when Robin and wife Glynis took over. Since then, the shop has gained a reputation for excellent quality, personal service and good value, and it is good to see that family traditions still apply in this business as their children Jonathan and Emily, along with an excellent team, take over the reins. Robin is still there to ensure these values are upheld!

Following the Family Tradition

Their small abattoir is one of the last of its kind in the county. Jonathan is now in complete control of the process of sourcing livestock and preparing it for sale.

The definition of a master butcher is a butcher who can select livestock, slaughter and dress a carcass, and display and offer for sale the cuts of meat. So Robin and Jonathan fit those criteria, giving you great peace of mind when buying your Sunday joint or any other of their meat products.

Whilst being able to purchase English lamb, beef, pork and poultry you will notice as you enter the shop an array of other products,

Jonathan and Emily
following the family tradition

many of which are made on the premises. There are delicious cakes, including Bakewell tarts and apple pies, meat pies of varying fillings, sausage rolls, and cheeses from around the country. Fresh vegetables are also on offer.

A variety of home-cooked dishes, with something to suit all tastes, including liver and onion, fish pie, braised steak in gravy, salmon and broccoli, sausage casserole, lasagne and many more. All are ready to heat through and eat in minutes. If that's not enough to tempt you, why not take your own dish and

have a pie or meal made for that special occasion? Now that's fresh!

Holloway Village Butchers also boasts the best view in Derbyshire, so if you care about meat as much as Robin and his staff do, take a ride out into the beautiful Derbyshire countryside and sample the delights of Derbyshire's premier butcher's shop where you will be greeted by a friendly smile and a hearty hello.

Contact Jonathan and Emily on 01629 534333 – local deliveries at no extra charge.

Bottled water with a twist!

Water is an essential nutrient that is involved in every function of the human body. You can live without food for several weeks, but will last less than seven days without water.

We lose about 250ml of water from our bodies each day just through breathing. To keep our bodies performing at their best, good hydration is essential – doctors and nutritionists recommend that we drink between six and eight 250ml glasses each day. But for most people getting to a tap regularly throughout the day isn't easy – and even if you can, it's not always that palatable.

But with fruity twists and a hint of the Derbyshire countryside, keeping a bottle of National Forest Spring Water at hand makes drinking a couple of litres a day a very easy medicine to swallow!

National Forest Spring Water is sourced from a 220ft-deep borehole on the edge of the Derbyshire town of Melbourne. The very name of the historic town is associated with water – it is derived from "mill on the brook". Throughout history the area has been associated with water and fertility. The town is situated just two miles from the River Trent. A few miles upstream this waterway continues to be used in the production of Burton-on-Trent's celebrated beers. Within a very short distance of Melbourne, reservoirs have now been created to take advantage of the area's wonderful hydration. However, the source of National Forest Spring Water stretches back in time. Geological studies have shown that it comes from gravel beds that could have been laid down by a river of the past.

The rich mix of geological attributes in the area – carboniferous limestone, millstone grit and alluvial floodplains included – have proved a fertile mix. Market gardening has long been a staple of the economy in the area; indeed, for many years water from the National Forest Spring was used to nourish delicious salad vegetables. More recently the area has become part of The National Forest, which aims to create a 200-square-mile area where woodland predominates. The region has always drawn lovers of the countryside and the outdoor life, and this new initiative is now bringing even more of them to the area.

National Forest Spring Water captures the flavours and goodness of the truly green environment it comes from. The water is inspired by and sourced in The National Forest – a natural attraction in the making that provides access to acres of countryside and the opportunity for countless rural leisure activities. National Forest Spring Water is fed from gravel beds 220ft beneath the surface on the edge of the historic Derbyshire town of Melbourne. It is bottled at source using state-of-the-art facilities. It comes still or sparkling – naturally pure – and is also available with a Forest Fruit flavour to add a sparkling fruity twist.

Look out for it in shops around the counties. Or, if you enjoy your water chilled and on tap, why not contact their vending department to see how little it costs to have a cooler.

For more information call 0800 169 7749

JAQUEST
Food Specialists

"REDWOOD" and "Farjals Country Foods" are brand names for the fish and meat products produced by John Jaquest and his wife Pauline. They specialise in extremely high quality food products and use only British produce where possible. This gives them an edge over their competition with quality and individuality!

Redwood Smokehouse is located in new premises on Bolsover's Business Park. Here you may watch as John Jaquest and his staff smoke their hams, bacon, venison, chicken, duck breast and salmon using age-old methods with oak and beech chippings. Redwood Smokery boasts award-winning chorizo sausages, smoked bacon, smoked roast salmon, smoked duck breast, ox tongue, pastrami, salt beef,

venison and kippers which all adorn the display cabinets.

John has won many awards for his great tasting food. The Guild of Fine Foods Great Taste awards awarded John Jaquest's homemade spicy chorizo the gold award for excellence, and many of his other products picked up silver medals. Gourmet-loving customers feast their eyes on food that can only be classed as five star. Jaquest now supplies, up to fifty hotels and restaurants throughout Derbyshire, Leicestershire, South Yorkshire and North Nottinghamshire.

He prepares his food, such as ham, bacon and pancetta, to his own recipe, and says the secret of his success has been his determination to only buy the best British produce. His smoked salmon comes from the Shetland Isles of Scotland, he uses Scottish Angus cross beef and locally reared pigs, duck and chicken. There are no artificial colours or preservatives in his foods,

and he only uses natural wood smoke, sea salt, raw cane sugar, herbs, spices and saltpetre, creating quality British food that tastes as good as it looks. John is assisted by his wife Pauline, who helps with the huge demand from the catering trade.

A visit to Redwood Smokehouse is a must for all good-food-loving connoisseurs.

Redwood Smokehouse,
Bolsover Business Park, off
Woodhouse Lane, Bolsover.
Derbyshire S44 6BD
Open 9am-5pm Monday to
Friday

Call 01246 827972 or email farjals@farjals.plus.com to place your order. All major cards accepted.

Ring 01246 827972 for trade inquiries. Free P & P on orders of over £100 within the British mainland excluding the Scottish Highlands, for orders between £50 and £100 P & P £8.00, and for smaller orders P & P £12.00. For deliveries to other destinations, price on application.

RICE

History

As a member of the grass family, rice has a fascinating history, possibly dating back as far as 3000BC. It needs both warmth and moisture to grow successfully, and grows up to two metres tall. Many countries are totally dependant on rice for their staple diet, and it is eaten by nearly half the world's population. It is non-allergenic and gluten free.

Cooking

In Britain, where Indian and Chinese cuisine have become some the nation's favourite foods, rice figures predominantly on the menu.

Rice is not difficult to cook but it is, without great care, possible to end up with clumps of it rather than the light fluffy food we set out to create. Below are a few tips for cooking successful rice.

Basic rules for successful rice

Generally we cook too much rice, and that's because we always seem to overlook the fact that rice triples in volume when cooked. Choosing an appropriately sized cooking utensil is vital.

- About 60g is sufficient for each person.

- Basmati and Thai rices need rinsing before cooking.

- Adhere strictly to the cooking times and quantities given on the packet. Don't just guess or you will end up with sticky rice.

- Always cook with the lid on. This prevents steam from escaping.

- Short rice clings together when cooking, but long grain rice is more fluffy.

- When the rice is cooked, do not serve straight onto the plate. Pour it into a colander and fluff it up with a fork.

There are two simple cooking methods – absorption and boiling.

Absorption

Take 1 part rice to 1.5 parts of water. Place rice in a colander and rinse. Put rice and a pinch of salt into the boiling water and bring back to the boil. Stir it well, cover with a tight-fitting lid, turn down to the lowest heat and leave for 12 minutes. Remove from heat; leave covered for a further 5 minutes to allow the moisture to be absorbed. Fluff with a fork.

Boiling

Add the rice to the boiling salted water. Bring back to the boil. Stir well, turn down the heat and cook for 10 minutes (check to ensure it is tender). Drain and then fluff with a fork.

There, that's all there is to it. Enjoy.

Things can only get better!

By Tony Maggs of The Honey Pot, Markeaton Park Craft Village.

As I start this year's article a lot has been happening in beekeeping; following years of petitions and letters to our MPs and the press and the public backing our campaign, the penny eventually dropped. Bees are important to our environment.

When the British banks were having a few problems balancing their books, billions of pounds were found to help them out in the crisis. But more importantly (in my opinion) the Government found a bit left over to help with the bee problems. The British Beekeepers Association need £1.6 million annually over the next five years, less than 1% of the £825 million of the value of the pollination provided by our bees to the UK economy over the last period. The Government found £4.3 million towards bee research and protection, a step in the right direction but much less than we asked for. When our bees have been having problems like the ones we have been experiencing, perhaps they are trying to tell us that something is not right. Until recently miners used to have a canary in a cage to take down the mine. If it kept on singing, the miners knew that the air was safe to breathe, but a dead canary told the miners to evacuate the mine immediately because there was a build-up of dangerous gases such as methane and carbon monoxide, to which the canary is sensitive. So I hope that the money can be used to help with the plight of the honey bee.

Other companies have made some positive steps too. The Co-op's Plan Bee is a good move, but I think most of the £150,000 will be spent on research on the pesticides used on farms. This is a good idea since some of us beekeepers and scientists think that some of the chemicals used in farming might be causing some of the problems. With the Co-op's Plan Bee, details of which can be found on their website, they are making a positive contribution.

There have been other companies helping out too. Rowse Honey have donated £100,000 towards bee research, and Professor Francis Ratnieks of Sussex University in conjunction with The Bee Farmers' Association will be working on a project to breed honeybees with better hygienic behaviours.

The WI are getting involved too. Tony Blair found out for himself what a formidable bunch of ladies they are – so Gordon Brown look out. The National Federation of Women's Institutes' Board is calling for beekeepers to receive, in the words of the Calendar Girls, "considerably bigger" funds. At their AGM in London on June 3, the WI will vote on the following resolution:

"SOS For Honey Bees: Honey Bees play a vital role in the pollination of food crops and in our environment. In view of concerns about the accelerating decline in the UK honey bee population, this meeting urges HM Government to increase funding for research into Bee Health."

With such a lot of new people wanting to learn the craft of beekeeping, "things can only get better."

Here in Derbyshire beekeeping has never been so popular, with about two hundred members and with sixty plus attending our regular monthly indoor meetings of the Derbyshire Beekeepers' Association, held at Crich (home to taste Derbyshire), with thanks to "The Bee Musketeers". This small team of experienced beekeepers film at an apiary the week before to show the members what to do for the month ahead. This is put together in a fun way, but the information is very well presented and appreciated.

More and more people are calling in at The Honey Pot at Markeaton Park Craft Village for advice on how to start beekeeping and buying all of the necessary beekeeping equipment. Who knows, maybe one day we will have enough beekeepers in our towns and villages to produce enough honey to stop having to import 95% of the honey

bought in Britain. We could enjoy beekeepers' local honey and, at the same time, ensure the welfare of the honey bee.

Here at The Honey Pot things have been difficult over the past year, with the bees' welfare taking precedence over honey production. The time and cost to sort out the bees and their equipment and to help the bees through a difficult time has been my priority in 2008; this caused me to run out of honey earlier this year, but with no colony losses this time to report, and a good start to 2009 and with a more "normal" winter and early spring, the weather has helped our bee colonies get off to a flying start this spring. Let's hope that a normal summer and autumn can follow too.

While I normally attend the Bakewell and Belper Farmers' Markets, they had to be put on hold earlier in the year due to the shortage of my Derbyshire Honey, but hopefully it will start flowing again at the end of May so that we can enjoy the early spring honey once more.

LOVE FOOD, LOVE GONALSTON FARM SHOP

Multi-award winning Gonalston Farm Shop (GFS) offers the finest quality local and British food plus a selection of delicacies from further afield.

Started in 2003 by Georgina and Ross Mason, GFS has gone from strength to strength winning a variety of accolades – one of eight finalists in the National Farm Retailer of the Year Award 2008, Nottinghamshire Small Business of the Year Winner 2006 – Evening Post Business Award, UK National Newcomer of the Year Winner 2005, Les Routiers accredited, and eleven Great Taste Awards for sausages.

FRESH FISH COUNTER – Following customer feedback we introduced our fresh fish counter in 2007, which offers an excellent selection of fresh fish to add to our range of smoked and frozen fish and shellfish. Fishmonger Dan Brazill, a trained and experienced chef, and his team are on hand to advise on every aspect of fish purchasing and preparation. Customers after something special can ring their order through in advance. A fish-preparation service is offered by Dan and his team.

ON-SITE BUTCHERY – With our roots firmly entrenched in farming history, our on-site butchery is proud to offer our beef reared on our own lush Trent Valley pastures, which is hung for a minimum of twenty-one days to mature and achieve optimum flavour. Our lamb and pork are raised by family farmers within an eight-mile radius of the shop, ensuring full traceability. We also offer a range of

quality British meats including over thirty varieties of our own recipe and award-winning sausages (including gluten free and low salt), poultry including fantastic free-range chickens from Packington Poultry in Staffordshire, seasonal game, gourmet speciality joints, freezer packs to order, dry cured bacon and hams, and our own produced BBQ range including many varieties of burgers, kebabs and marinated meats.

DELI – Our deli boasts the finest charcuterie including genuine Parma ham and Suffolk salami, beautiful cheeses such as our delicious local Stilton, and original 24-month aged Parmeggiano Reggiano as well as an olive bar to rival the best. We also offer a mouth-watering range of local patés, pork pies, ploughmans and game pies, award-winning hams and cooked meats.

FRUIT AND VEG – Throughout all the seasons of the year GFS always has a glorious array of salads, vegetables and fruit – delivered fresh every day and sourced locally where possible.

We also offer food lovers fresh breads, home-baked cakes, fine wines, beers, bespoke hampers and gift vouchers.

OUR ENVIRONMENT – Wherever possible our products are locally grown and highlighted with our fifty-food-mile stickers, enabling our customers to see at a glance that many of the finest quality local and British products are sourced within a fifty-food-mile radius, thereby reducing food miles travelled.

Another way GFS care for the

environment is by encouraging customers to reuse their own shopping bag; we actively incentivise this by deducting a penny off the bill for every bag reused, be it one of ours or somebody else's. Customers are also able to bring their egg boxes back to the shop for re-filling.

LOYALTY – We believe that loyalty should be rewarded and we run our GFS Fresh Loyalty Card whereby customers receive one point per £1 spent on virtually all products in the store. As well as receiving our quarterly newsletter, Loyalty Card holders are also eligible for our regular points offers throughout the store.

As a one-stop shop for all food lovers, we look forward to being of service to you.

TV celebrity chef Lesley Waters, a strong campaigner for local seasonal and sustainable British produce, says: "Gonalston Farm Shop is one of the most inspiring farm shops I have ever visited."

Gonalston Farm Shop, Southwell Road, Gonalston, Nottinghamshire NG14 7DR, www.gonalstonfarmshop.co.uk Email: info@gonalstonfarmshop.co.uk. Open Tuesday to Saturday 9am to 6.30pm, Sundays 10am to 4pm, Bank Holidays 10am to 4pm, otherwise closed Mondays.

Dairy Products Now at Redgates

The Redgate family have been farming in the Brinsley area of Nottinghamshire for nearly two hundred years, and four generations have been farming at Coney Grey Farm.

Jean and David Redgate are proud to introduce to their customers old and new their newly refurbished farm shop which now boasts a newly installed extension to house their current produce and their already extensive delicatessen range. New to the farm shop is the sale of milk, cream, yoghurts and butter (provided by Peak District Dairy at Tideswell, Derbyshire).

The farm shop will soon be stocking a range of bakery products which will include bread, pastries and cakes so watch this space!

Master butcher Peter Redgate offers a full range of butchery services and will gladly help customers with their meat and catering requirements, from a simple barbeque to a larger function.

The farm shop supplies the local comprehensive school with produce for their school dinners, and is proud to be educating children from local schools in healthy eating.

To appreciate their high quality produce why not pay them a visit? For all enquiries and opening times telephone 01773 713403 or visit them at Redgates Farm Shop, Coney Grey Farm, Mansfield Road, Brinsley, Nottinghamshire. NG165AE

Naturally Reared, Naturally Better

A visit to Scaddows family-run Farm Shop and café overlooking their PYO fruit fields and beautiful surrounding countryside is a treat indeed.

Here they grow their own strawberries, raspberries, blackcurrants and gooseberries; there are available in the shop, or you can pick-your-own during the summer from mid-June, as well as their own delicious asparagus which is ready in mid-April. They offer a range that is delicious, home-grown, local, and conscientiously farmed. This includes fruit and veg from 'South Derbyshire Growers', meat from their award-winning butcher Peter Coates, local cheese and local home-made jams, chutneys, cakes and other goodies.

Their café serves a range of snacks and light meals, all freshly prepared and including home-made specials such as their very popular delicious soups, quiches and cakes.

Scaddows Farm Shop aims to supply high quality local products with the finest possible value, together with friendly, personal service. You will always be assured of a great atmosphere, a friendly welcome and individual service when you visit.
Scaddows Farm Shop, Ticknall, Derby DE73 7JP.
Telephone: 01332 865709
www.scaddowsfarm.co.uk
Opening times are: Mon–Fri 8.30–5.30, Sat 8.30–4.30 and Sun 10–4

ROYAL APPROVAL FOR ORGANIC STORE

A ROYAL thumbs-up for two Derby women heralded the start of a business success story and one of Derbyshire's most unique retail experiences.

Just days before Rachel Done-Johnson and Sandra Hill launched Oliver's Organics, in Duffield Road, Allestree, in September 2008,

the pair received an official correspondence from Prince Charles. In the letter, which was signed on behalf of The Prince of Wales by his private secretary Elizabeth Buchanan, the heir to the throne sent the pair his best wishes, hoping "the shop will be a great success."

Since the store was opened by Derby Mayor Councillor Barbara Jackson it has gone from strength to strength. Initially focusing on Fair Trade and organic beauty therapy, wine, retail, coffee and cupcakes, the store has now branched out into locally-supplied produce as well. Recent developments include the introduction of a deli counter and a range of chocolates made by Derbyshire-based chocolate makers.

Mrs Done-Johnson said: "It's been a wonderful first six months for us – the support we've had has been incredible."

The White Post Farm Shop
Farnsfield, Notts

The White Post Farm Shop opened in the summer of 2007. Local Michelin-starred chef Sat Bains was on hand to cut the ribbon and sample some of the fresh produce. Bains was the perfect dignitary to open the shop with its ethos placed firmly on local produce for our local customers.

As the shop has grown over the last two years the philosophy has remained the same, and the shop now boasts some of the finest produce that Nottinghamshire has to offer: bread from Atherleys Bakery in Farnsfield, cakes and pastries from Sally Jane's in Norwell, amazing chilli products from the Gringley Gringo, Beryl's Honey from Newark and now a fantastic range of real ales from a number of local microbreweries, Milestone Brewery in Cromwell, Newark, Oldershaw Brewery in Grantham, Springhead in Newark and Castle Rock in Nottingham. Each brewery offers a generous range of real ales, stouts and lagers with a flavour to please the most discerning of palates.

Perhaps the proudest element of the White Post Farm Shop is the home-bred meat. With over twenty years of experience in animal husbandry, the farm ensures the highest possible welfare standards. Traditional breeds of pork and lamb enjoy free range of the paddocks, creating a product for which the White Post Farm Shop has become renowned.

The shop now supplies local pubs and restaurants with its own pork and lamb, yet can still maintain the lowest prices for its much valued customers. Customers can also enjoy beef reared only a few paddocks from the site, and a fascinating range of alternative frozen meats: ostrich, bison, kangaroo and more.

As with all the retail outlets at White Post Farm, the Farm Shop, Farnsfield, Notts is free to enter, so pop in and taste some of this fine local produce for yourself, or phone and speak to Jenny on 01623 883847.

Two hundred years of Denby's stoneware pots

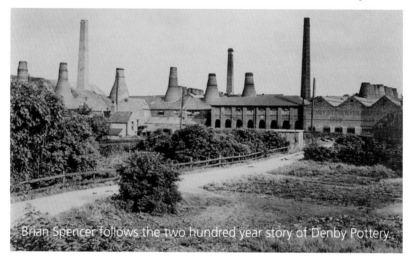

Brian Spencer follows the two hundred year story of Denby Pottery.

Derbyshire has long been a useful source of the raw materials needed for making stoneware pottery, those everyday functional utensils that have been the mainstay of kitchens up and down the land. Luckily the special clay used for stoneware is found in close proximity to coal measures, which in the early days of pottery production was an essential fuel for firing kilns. In 1808, during the construction of the Alfreton to Derby turnpike, dual seams of coal and clay were uncovered at Denby.

William Bourne, a potter from nearby Belper, was summoned to examine the clay and immediately recognised its fine qualities. Though tied to his work at Belper Pottery, William decided that with his guidance his son Joseph, although still in his early twenties, should be given the task of operating a pottery at Denby. In 1809 a small group of sheds and pot banks, the unique bottle-shaped pottery kilns, grew close to the handily situated beds of clay. Local labour no doubt trained by Belper-based potters soon took on the skills needed, and the only commodity that had to be brought in was salt to give the pots their distinctive glaze. However, as there was already a steady flow

Joseph Bourne

Sarah Elizabeth Bourne

of salt carried by teams of pack ponies between Cheshire and south Yorkshire, it would have been no problem diverting loads from the traditional west-east traffic through the Peak District.

Through the entrepreneurial skills of young Joseph Bourne, the pottery at Denby prospered and soon built up an international reputation for the quality of its pots and jars. In the early nineteenth century glass was still expensive, and stoneware jars were the essential alternative to hold commodities such as preserves, pickles, ink, polish, ginger beer and mineral water. The distinctive brown mottled colour of these jars was created by shovelfuls of salt thrown into the kiln during the firing process. Not only did the salt give the pots their unique colour, but it also created a strengthening glaze. An ambitious man with commercial acumen, Joseph was also an innovator who patented many of his ideas for improved firing methods in salt glaze kilns.

The name Denby Pottery did not come into being for many years, and for a long time the pottery was known by the family name of Bourne, who ran the business effectively until 1942. Joseph, the founder, died aged 71 in 1860, and his son Joseph Harvey Bourne followed him but sadly had little time to prove he was a worthy successor to his father since he died some nine years later. At a time when women were expected to stay at home, Joseph Harvey's widow, Sarah Elizabeth

Bourne, stepped in and successfully ran the business for the next thirty years. Under her guidance the company continued to prosper and widened its product range to include decorated artware, and also extended its ranges of kitchenware. Spotting a brand new market in the then infant telephone and telegraphic network, the pottery became one of the main producers of telegraphic insulators, those squat round pots that still carry telephone wires around telegraph poles.

Sadly Joseph and Sarah had no children to pass the thriving business on to, and following her death in 1898 control of the pottery was handed to two nephews, one from either side of Joseph and Sarah's marriage. Sarah's own nephew withdrew from the business in 1907, leaving a third Joseph – Joseph Bourne Wheeler – as the sole proprietor. In 1916 Denby Pottery was formed into a limited liability company with Joseph Bourne Wheeler as Governing Director – a post he held until his death in 1942.

Danesby Ware
ELECTRIC BLUE

Joseph Bourne
& Son, Limited
Denby Pottery, Nr. Derby

London Office & Showroom:
54, HOLBORN VIADUCT, E.C.1

With glass becoming less expensive and more useful for holding liquids, Denby turned away from making stoneware bottles and jars, concentrating on kitchenware while at the same time improving the artistic attraction of its pots. Moving ahead of its competitors who tried to keep to the old salt glazed

Glyn Colledge

products, the firm's innovative ranges such as Cottage Blue and Manor Green were an immediate success and remained in production for over fifty years. Unfortunately the war put these attractive designs on hold for the duration, and the firm was forced to concentrate on industrial ware such as telegraphic insulators and battery jars. Denby Pottery was only allowed to make one range during the war years, called, with bureaucratic lack of imagination, 'Utility Brown'. Many of the massive dark brown tea pots dispensing NAAFI 'char' were made by the firm, along with large stoneware jugs to hold sailors' rum rations.

With the post-war removal of petty restrictions, Denby soon got into its stride once more and began selling ranges of tableware patterns that pushed the firm to the fore in ceramic design. Along with a range of jugs and bowls sold under the brand name 'Glynware' after their designer, Glyn Colledge, one of a team considered to be amongst the best in the trade, Denby went on to produce a series of designs that were to become popular. Designs such as 'Greenwheat', 'Chevron' and 'Studio' became an instant hit and are still the pride of many

kitchens up and down the land. Not a firm to rest on its laurels, Denby spearheaded a new concept in tableware called 'oven-to-tableware', with ranges such as 'Arabesque' at the forefront of the idea. This combination of good design and durability avoided the need to transfer food from cooking pots to ornate tableware dishes.

The firm's success continued to grow, especially with its breakthrough into the US market, and in 1970 the company was floated on the London Stock Exchange. While this improved Denby's cash-flow it did however bring it to the attention of larger firms looking for ways of expanding their empire. In 1981 Denby's shares were acquired by Crown House Engineering and the pottery joined the group's other tableware manufacturers, including Edinburgh Crystal, Thomas Webb Crystal, George Butler Cutlery and Dema Glass from Chesterfield. In 1987 the tableware companies within the Crown House group were taken over by the home furnishings conglomerate Coloroll, who put a strong management team into Denby.

Unfortunately Coloroll's over-ambitious expansion policies led to its downfall, but as Denby Pottery was still in a viable position, its management team arranged a buyout. With their design and management skills the firm continued to prosper with best-selling ranges such as 'Imperial Blue' and 'Regency Green' leading the list of popular lines. However, it soon became obvious that in order to install up-to-date plant and equipment, Denby would need yet more capital. As a result a new company was floated on the London Stock Exchange at a time when Denby's turnover had more than doubled (from

£10.7m in 1990/91 to £21.9m in 1993/94). In 1999 external factors prompted the Denby team to return the company into private ownership through yet another management buyout, helped initially by Phildrew Ventures, a speculative finance concern, and then subsequently by the Bank of Scotland. Approaching its bicentenary and with a turnover now around £38m, Denby Pottery has recently been taken over by Valco Capital Partners, as another means of injecting ever-necessary capital into the pottery.

With two hundred years of proud history behind it, Denby Pottery has launched a commemorative tableware range called 'Natural Pearl'. This will join their new generation of 'Iconic Classics', a range with lustrous, pearlescent tones and round curvy shapes. The range has a natural, organic feel, creating a premium tableware range suitable for both formal and informal dining.

For a firm established by Joseph Bourne, a young man in his early twenties sent in 1809 by his father to the tiny hamlet of Denby in order to exploit the newly discovered deposits of clay, Denby Pottery Company can rightfully claim its position amongst the major successes of our region.

HIGHFIELD HOUSE FARM SHOP

Highfield House farm shop at Stonedge is a family concern with genuine family values. David and Sylvia Prince first opened the shop doors in 1998.

On my visit I was greeted by Matthew – David and Sylvia's son. Matthew joined the business in 2004 having had a very successful career in retailing. He decided that whatever you do in a corporate company, more is always wanted, so he decided to use his energies and talents in the family firm instead.

Matthew gave me the history of the business: David and Sylvia bought the farm in 1986 but only had a limited knowledge of farming. However, what they did have was bags of enthusiasm and plenty of energy.

They set up with a small flock of mules put to Texel and Suffolk Tups. Over the next few years cattle and pigs were introduced, and in 1990, the Hightecs Texel flock was introduced. It is clear from this that expansion was on their minds, and the obvious way to do this was to move into

retail, hence, the shop opened in 1998. Over the next eight years the business grew steadily as their reputation for quality produce spread around the county.

Soon, with an established and happy client base, Highfield House farm shop was ready for expansion and a grant was obtained to transform and expand the farm shop to what you see today. This coincided with Matthew joining the family business.

They also purchased the remainder of the oldest Suffolk flock in Derbyshire, the Bubnell flock. From these twenty-four ewes and the stock ram they have developed their flock to give sheep of great size and performance. Still on the sheep theme, they purchased six Beltex ewes to produce the Stonedge Beltex

flock. The experience gained over this period of time has helped to develop Highfield House farm shop into a thriving business with in-depth knowledge of their produce, most of which is grown and sourced locally. Added to that is their trade side, supplying to local restaurants, cafés and public houses.

Plans are now afoot to develop a bakehouse, which will give the delightful smell of freshly baked produce as you walk through the door. A visit to this well-stocked farm shop will certainly afford you the opportunity to buy quality produce from a family business with local expertise.

As we were finishing our chat David arrived back from his trade deliveries. We quickly got the staff together for a photograph, and David certainly was the life and soul of the party. He has a sharp sense of humour and got everyone smiling for the picture.

Pictured are: back row: David, Alan and Matthew. Front row: Rachel and Adrian.

Their website contains recipes which link in with their produce. One of the more popular recipes - Lamb Shanks - is reproduced here.

Highfield House Farm, B5057 Darley Road, Stonedge, Ashover, Chesterfield, Derbyshire S45 0LW

Open Monday – Saturday 8–5. Sunday 10–2
www.highfieldhousefarm.co.uk
matthew@highfieldhousefarm.co.uk
01246 590817; 01246 591327

Highfield House Farm Lamb Shanks with Horseradish and Rosemary

Feeds: 2
Time to cook: Approximately 2–2½ hours
Oven temperature: Gas mark 3, 160°C, 325°F

Ingredients
Lamb shanks
Oil
Garlic
Onion
Carrot
Celery stalks
Horseradish sauce or fresh horseradish
Tomato passata
Stock
Fresh rosemary stalks
Baby potatoes

Method
Heat 15ml (1tbsp) oil in a large frying pan, add 2 lamb shanks and fry until golden all over (approx 10 minutes). Add 2 cloves garlic (crushed), 1 onion (chopped), 1 carrot (chopped), 2 celery stalks (sliced), 30ml (2tbsp) horseradish sauce or fresh horseradish (grated), and stir together.

Pour over 400g tomato passata and 300ml stock and bring to boil. Season. Pour into a casserole dish, add 2 large fresh rosemary stalks.

Cover and cook for 1½ hours (or alternatively this can be slowly simmered on the hob).

Add 450g baby potatoes (scrubbed), making sure they are covered by the liquid. Continue cooking for a further 30–45 minutes until potatoes are tender and the meat is falling from the bone.

Serve with stir-fried Savoy cabbage.

Eat.

JERRY HOWARTH
Pork Butchers

In 1898 Jeremiah Howarth launched his butchery business on High Street in Belper. Since that moment a success story has unfolded with three generations of Jeremiahs and one Tim taking a small family Pork Butchers to international renown.

Tim Howarth (left) and Robert Montgomery at the King Street shop

Each generation has brought with it new flair and innovation. In fact, as is often the case in family businesses, the son has great ideas for change and the father resists! This was true in the Howarths' case too, as Mrs Mavis Howarth explained to me. When her husband Jerry, Jeremiah's grandson, joined the business he had some great ideas but his father wasn't too keen, and that scenario repeated itself when her son Tim went into the business and took over from his father. Jerry had to concede that he too had been in that position, and decided that it was best to listen to his son just as his father had.

Jerry was the fourth child of the family and as a lad he used to breed pigs. He was only five when his dad sat him on the end of the counter and taught him to link sausages. All his holidays were spent working in the business. This work ethic has continued with Tim who, each weekend, used to spend his time working at the shop. This stood him in good stead, because in 2001, after his father

Jerry retired after a heart bypass operation, he was able to take over the business.

The King Street shop soon became a vital part of the town business community; it is now under the careful eye of Robert Montgomery who joined the business in 2001. The High Street premises now house

the successful factory which makes all the produce for the shops. These include pies, sausages, haggis (in season), haslet, polony, oatcakes and much more.

Everything is under the careful eye of Tim, and Mavis is still around to make sure all is well. She explained that retiring is not something she really wanted to do; she has enjoyed having more time to herself, but she still enjoys going into work to do the paperwork and wages. During her time she has done most jobs in the business, including boning the chops, organising outdoor barbecues and running the shop. Since Jerry sadly died in November 2008 Mavis still goes in to help out and enjoys her time in the business.

Tim's son Ashley now works in the business, so the family tradition looks set to continue. This thriving retail and wholesale Pork Butchers has been part of Belper life for over a hundred years, and even with new supermarkets muscling their way into Belper

it continues to grow and succeed. This is due to the late Jerry Howarth's motto, which the family holds to today – 'I won't give customers anything I can't eat myself'.

Quality is and always has been paramount at Howarth's. Why not try it yourself?

Jerry Howarth,
7 King Street,
Belper,
Derbyshire DE56 1PW
01773 822557

The late Jerry Howarth – mentor of the family firm.

Grow Your Own

The allotment has made quite a comeback recently. They are being snapped up quickly.
Many TV programmes are encouraging those with a small garden area to have a go at growing their own vegetables. Not only is it a cost-effective way of eating, it is satisfying as well as healthy.

What could be better than nipping out into the garden and cutting yourself a fresh lettuce, or having a whole supply of onions for the year nicely tucked away?

Raised Beds

Raised bed gardening is becoming increasingly popular due to the fact that they drain well and are ideal if you have poor soil. They can be placed on a patio, terrace or on your bare soil.
They are easy to make using tanalised timber in a size to suit the position you require it in. They should be 15cm deep on soil and 25cm deep on a patio. They are ideal for growing most vegetables and salads. If you want to go further you can use sleepers, which really do give you ample space for an extensive vegetable plot.

Growbags

Growbags have been a popular way of growing tomatoes for many years, but they are a versatile way of growing lettuce, cress, spring onions, beetroot and so on.

On the next page are a few vegetables that you can grow and their planting and reaping times.

Vegetable Growing Calendar

	Sow	Plant	Harvest
Asparagus	Jan-Feb	Apr-May	Apr-June
Carrot	Jan-Aug	June-Mar	
Cauliflower	Jan-June	Mar-July	All year round
Brussels Sprout	Feb-Apr	Apr-May	Aug-Mar
Celeriac	Feb-Apr	Apr-May	Oct-Dec
Celery	Feb-May	Mar-Jun	Jul-Nov
Lettuce (outdoor)	Feb onwards	Apr onwards	Jun onwards
Onion (salad)	Feb-Jun		Jun-Nov
Onion (bulbing)	Feb-Apr		Aug-Oct
Parsley	Feb-Jul & Sep		June & April onwards
Parsnip	Feb-Apr		Oct-Feb
Peas (sugar)	Feb-May		Jun-Sept
Rhubarb	Feb-May		2nd year
Rocket (varies to variety)	Feb-Sep		3-4 wks
Potatoes (early)	Mar-Apr		Jun-July
Radish (outdoor)	Mar-Aug		Jun-Nov
Squash/Courgettes/Marrow	Mar-Apr	May-Jun	Jun-Sept
Turnip	Mar-Aug		Jun-Nov
Leek	Mar-May	Apr-May	Jul-Apr
Beetroot	Mar-Jul		Jun-Oct
Cabbage (winter)	Apr-May	May-Jun	Oct onwards
Cabbage (savoy)	Apr-May	May-Jun	Oct onwards
Swede	Apr-Jun		Sep-Mar
Sweetcorn	Apr-Jun		Aug-Oct
Squash (pumpkin)	Apr-Jun	May	Jul-Oct
Broccoli (sprouting)	Apr-Jun	Jun-July	July-May
Beans (French climbing)	May-Jun		Jul-Oct
Beans (runner)	May-Jun		Jul-Oct
Kale	May-Jul	Jun-Aug	Oct-Feb
Potatoes (late)	Jun-Jul		Sept-Oct
Sweet Potato	Jun-Jul		Sept-Oct
Strawberry	Oct-Nov & Dec-Jan		May onwards
Aubergine (indoor)	Nov-Feb	Jan-Apr	April onwards
Beans (broad)	Nov & Feb-May		May to Oct
Peas	Nov & Mar-Jun		May & Jun-Sept
Tomato (indoor)	Nov-Mar	Jan-May	Aug-Oct
Peppers (indoor)	Dec-Apr	Feb-Jun	Apr-Oct
Lettuce (indoor)	All year round		All year round

Grow Your Own

ROSEMARY

The fresh and dried leaves are used frequently in traditional Mediterranean cuisine; they have a bitter, astringent taste, which complements a wide variety of foods. A tisane can also be made from them. When burned they give off a distinct mustard smell, as well as a smoky smell which can be used to flavour foods while barbecuing.

Rosemary is extremely high in iron, calcium, and Vitamin B6.

DILL

Fresh dill's fernlike leaves are aromatic. A sprig of dill will perk up most soups, salads and main dishes. It is quite easy to grow even within a small garden, giving you regular access to this versatile herb. Dill is best used when fresh, as it can lose its flavour rapidly if dried. You can, however, freeze-dry the leaves and preserve their flavour, but don't leave them too long as fresh is best. Dill seed is used as a spice, with a flavour somewhat similar to caraway, but also resembling that of fresh or dried dill weed.

MINT

What on earth would spring lamb be without a sprinkle of mint? As with dill, you can grow this yourself - but beware, it is a fast grower and can become a nuisance, so choose an area that you don't mind it taking over. Mint is used to flavour sauces, soups, fish, meat, poultry and stews. Peppermint is good for teas and spearmint for meat sauces.

TARRAGON

If you like a spot of Béarnaise sauce on your food, then you will like tarragon since it is the main ingredient. A member of the daisy family, fresh tarragon is stronger than dried so be mindful of this when using it! Too much will overpower your sauces. It has a slight liquorice flavour. You can freeze it and use it straight from frozen. Sauces made from tarragon can be used as dips for fish dishes such as shrimps or even meat and chicken.

You can grow tarragon if you have well-drained soil. It also loves lots of sun.

BAY LEAF

The bay leaf is probably the most commonly used herb in the kitchen. It has a rich history originating in Asia Minor. The bay laurel tree loves a warm climate. One of the greatest exporters of bay leaves is Turkey. The taste is slightly floral, but if eaten whole the leaf is quite bitter. Bay leaves are used in soups, meat stews, seafood and vegetable dishes.

CINNAMON

The earliest recorded use of cinnamon is in the Bible book of Exodus, so we are talking in excess of 3500 years ago. Cinnamon was an expensive product and was given as a gift to monarchs. People put cinnamon in apple pie – a sin in our book! Cinnamon bark is used as a spice. Cinnamon buns are to die for, and chicken and lamb dishes come to life with a touch of cinnamon.

HORSERADISH

Horseradish is worth its weight in gold according to Greek mythology. It was known in Egypt in 1500BC. The grated root of horseradish is mixed with vinegar to produce quite a potent condiment. Try adding a little to soup; it really spices it up.

OREGANO

If you enjoy Italian and Greek cuisine it will not have escaped your notice that they feature oregano heavily. It works in an opposite way to dill in that it is stronger dried than fresh. It is better when linked with hot and spicy foods, especially pizza, which is where it is really at home and has been for centuries.
It has an aromatic, warm and slightly bitter taste.

Infusiastic
idea for tea!

When is a tea not a tea?

When it's a herb tea, of course. So, using the word tea is totally inappropriate when describing an infusion made from purely herbs!

Officially it's a tisane, or ptisan which is a herbal infusion made by infusing things such as nettles, rosehip, rosemary, sage and so on. However, it is possible to have herb tea because some teas are infused with herbs too!

Tisane have many uses, and over the years they have gained popularity due to their medicinal properties. If you read any of the Peter Rabbit books you will know that Peter's mother gives him a dose of chamomile tea after a particularly busy day spent in a watering can.

Tea can be mixed with herbs, and these have become quite popular as an afternoon refresher. Teas such as Earl Grey, possibly named after a British Prime Minister (Charles Grey) who, apparently received a gift of tea flavoured with bergamot, now hold great sway in the tea world. Why, even Captain Picard of Star Trek fame drinks it! He even orders it in a kind of French accent.

Peppermint tisane is most refreshing and has the ability to ease an upset stomach. Try this simple recipe and enjoy a refreshing herb tea.

200g peppermint leaves
200g lemon balm leaves
200g fennel seeds

Mix the herbs thoroughly and place in an airtight container. When you feel like a drink just use 1 teaspoon in a cup of boiling water and steep for 10 minutes before straining off the herbs.

Food Hygiene

Millions of people in the UK suffer from food poisoning every year, but many cases of food poisoning could be prevented by following a few simple food hygiene tips.

Preparing food

Bacteria spreading from one food to another is a major cause of food poisoning. This can happen when raw food touches or drips onto ready-to-eat food, or when chopping boards, utensils and people's hands have touched raw food. To prevent bacteria from spreading, remember to do the following:

❏ always wash your hands before preparing food and after touching raw food, especially raw meat
❏ prepare raw and ready-to-eat food separately
❏ if you have used a knife or chopping board with raw meat, do not use them with ready-to-eat food (such as fruit, salad and cooked food) unless you have cleaned them thoroughly first
❏ keep cloths, tea towels and hand towels clean and change them frequently

Cooking food

Cooking food properly kills harmful bacteria. It's important to do the following:

❏ thaw meat and poultry fully before cooking
❏ always check that food is piping hot all the way through before you eat it, even if you have followed a recipe or cooking instructions on packaging
❏ don't reheat food more than once and always check that it is piping hot all the way through before you eat it

Chilling food

Some foods need to be kept chilled to keep them safe; for example, food with a 'use by' date, food that you have cooked and will not serve immediately, or other ready-to-eat food such as prepared salads.

Always remember to:

❏ put food that needs to be chilled in the fridge straight away
❏ cool cooked food as quickly as possible and then put it in the fridge
❏ store raw meat and poultry in a sealed container at the bottom of the fridge to stop it touching or dripping onto ready-to-eat food
❏ don't overload the fridge – this can stop cold air from circulating, which could allow foods to get too warm

Take extra care

If you are preparing food for elderly people, babies, toddlers, pregnant women or someone who is ill, avoid giving them eggs with runny yolks, or foods that contain eggs that won't be cooked, for example, homemade mayonnaise and some types of ice cream, icing or mousse. This is because eggs can contain harmful bacteria. When preparing eggs for these people, cook them until the white and yolk are solid.

The Wok

a chef's most versatile kitchen utensil

The wok is a round-bottomed cooking vessel which has its origins in China.

It is mainly used for stir-frying, but, and here is the beauty of this utensil, it can also be used in loads of different ways, such as stewing, frying, braising, steaming, deep frying, boiling water, smoking, or even making soup.

Its shape and long handle make it easy for the chef to toss the food around for fast cooking at high temperatures without it getting burnt. The shape allows a hot spot at the bottom for fast efficient cooking and also allows food to drop from the sides into the centre thus taking away the frustrations of contemporary pans where you have to chase the food around.

You also need to be mindful of the weight of the wok. You may need to get into training before you use one, especially if it's cast iron! Good wrist and arm muscles are required. If you need one a little lighter you can buy carbon steel woks. However, it is good to bear in mind that cast iron woks retain the heat longer and are therefore more efficient.

Buying a good quality wok is essential, because when cooking at high temperatures ones made from cheaper material can tend to 'warp'. This makes it impossible for them to 'sit' well on the stove. Better quality woks are generally hand-hammered and made from two sheets of carbon steel. For a round-bottomed wok to sit on your stove it may be necessary to purchase a wok ring.

Help for the Honey Bee with Plan BEE

By Janet Smith

'I eat my peas with honey;
I've done so all my life.
It makes the peas taste funny.
But it keeps them on my knife.'

Spike Milligan

The busy buzzing of bees as they investigate flower after flower is as inseparable from summer as the birds' dawn chorus is from spring, but the honeybee is in trouble. Some supermarkets cannot even obtain English honey. Honeybees are dying in great numbers; one in three (240,000) hives were lost last year, and it is not understood why. But the problem extends beyond honey, because a third of the food we eat, from cucumber to zucchini, apple to coriander, turnip to sweet cherry and pear to rosehip, is pollinated by honeybees. Apart from a growing silence in our gardens, they are worth £165 million to the UK economy. Tim Lovett, President of the British Bee Keeping Association, says that to replicate what the bee does would take a workforce of thirty million people.

The list of suspects for their decline ranges from the varroa mite to loss of habitat, and from bad weather to urban sprawl. One theory is that in an effort to breed a productive and yet docile bee, genetic narrowing has occurred, resulting in a less hardy insect. Another theory is that they are affected by neonicotinoids, a pesticide group restricted in Europe but not here. In an effort to reverse the fortunes of the bee, the UK's largest farmer, the Co-operative Group with twenty-one farms covering 25,000 hectares, is banning the eight suspect pesticides from their fresh produce. The

Plan BEE

Co-op symbol of a bee on a honeycomb, representing working together for the greater good, is being used to launch their rescue package – aptly named Plan Bee.

Flowering plants and their pollinators are thought to have evolved in parallel 120 million years ago. Relatively recently the oldest bee fossil in the world was discovered in Burma; this bee has been trapped inside its time capsule of tree resin (amber) for 100 million years. Paul Monaghan, head of social goals at the Co-op, said, 'Nature's number one pollinating machine appears to be breaking down and no one knows for sure why. But it's not just pretty gardens that are at stake; one third of the average diet relies on honeybees. Recently the Government finally accepted that there was a problem (£4.3 million towards research and protection). However, we are still not seeing any real recognition that pesticides could be a contributory factor. The great thing, though, is that we can all do our bit to turn things around. Whether it's a lush rural retreat or a tiny urban window box, we can plant and garden in ways that help the honeybee thrive. At the Co-operative we have more than three million members and we hope to educate and empower them to be ambassadors for Plan Bee."

One aim is to encourage people to set aside an area of long grass and to plant wild flowers in their gardens. To kick-start the scheme they are giving away 20,000 free packets of wild flower seeds to members. Subsidized bee shelters have also been sourced, and the Co-op are adding £150,000 towards research. A three-year project on their farms aims to identify the best mix of wild flowers to plant in field margins and set-aside land to attract and support honeybees. Also at forty locations around the UK, a new film raising awareness of the global decline of honeybees is being shown to Co-operative members, prior to its general release.

If things are bad here, the US honeybee is in dire straits, suffering from what's known as colony collapse disorder where bees abandon hives wholesale, deserting the queen and the young. There are also problems in France, Germany, Italy, Spain, Greece, Brazil and Argentina. In southern Sichuan, China, where the honeybee population was wiped out by uncontrolled use of pesticides, pear trees now have to be pollinated by hand.

Tips for a bee friendly garden include: the provision of a shallow-edged dish of water with pebbles for easy access and to prevent drowning; densely planting an area of flowerbed for shelter in bad weather; eliminating or reducing pesticides by encouraging natural predators such as ladybirds, lacewings, frogs, hedgehogs and birds; spraying with a light soap solution is also useful for removing aphids and similar pests, as are deterrents and barriers. Flowers attractive to bees include alyssum, goldenrod, French marigold, candytuft, sunflower, thistle, cornflower, common poppy, dahlias, sweet william, chives (flowering heads), lesser snapdragon and many more. An even more pro-active way to help bees is to join the band of 44,000 UK beekeepers. Those near Co-operative farms are encouraged to keep their hives on Co-op farmland.

Worldwide there are 20,000 varieties of bees, but only a handful are honeybees. They are not the only pollinators; other insects, such as butterflies, moths, flies and beetles, and also birds and the wind play their part in helping plants produce fruit. Honeybees also pollinate plants that line watercourses and prevent erosion. Visiting flower after flower, they leave behind a few specks of golden pollen which results in cross-pollination of plants; this is better than self-pollination, as inbreeding may be undesirable, or may not produce seeds, because the development of different parts of the same flower are not always in harmony.

Many plants have their own particular pollinators; the macadamia nut, marrow, pawpaw and kiwi fruit, for example, are totally reliant on the honeybee, whilst starfruit, coriander, turnip,

apricot and apple are mostly reliant. Coconut and coffee, on the other hand, need only a modest input from them.

Bees are dependent upon flowers for their diet of pollen and nectar. The different nectars collected by the bees during the seasons are reflected in the flavours and shades of the honeys; oilseed rape in the spring, then on to the bean-fields. July brings borage honey, and sunflower. Later many beekeepers pack up their hives and transport them to the moors for the white and purple heather.

Honey is basically ripened nectar containing pure sugars, and the life of the bee is dedicated to its production. Essentially it is for themselves and their young, but they vastly over-cater. Each honeybee hive contains around 50,000 bees. Most are female workers, but it is the queen bee, raised on royal jelly, who is the mother of them all; she can lay an astounding two thousand eggs a day. Whilst a queen can live several years, a worker lasts only a matter of weeks. In a lifetime a worker bee plays many roles, from queen attendant to nurse, and from guard to field worker. Male drones number only a few hundred, and lead a less varied life; they are summarily despatched by the workers at the end of the season.

In addition to being a

source of energy used in food and drink, including mead, that pick-me-up for monks, honey has long been acclaimed for its healing properties. Today if one suffers from a leg ulcer, the nurse may well apply a honey and paraffin dressing. In ancient Egypt it was used in the process of embalming mummies. Beeswax, a by-product of honey, when mixed with paraffin makes fine furniture polish.

Beeswax candles, still much in use today, create little smoke. Formerly they were only for the wealthy; the poor burned candles of rendered fat. In early beekeeping the bees were kept in a wicker basket or a conical straw skep. Unhappily for them, when the time came to harvest the honey they were often killed by holding the hive over sulphurous fumes. Gradually new designs with removable parts enabled colonies to be kept, and breeding became by selection rather than by fortune.

The British black bee or Apis mellifera (apis is Latin for bee, mel is honey and fluere means flow) was decimated by disease in the 1930s, but there are moves to re-introduce it. A popular bee with beekeepers is the Italian bee because of its even temper, although they are now under a spotlight as they may not be robust enough for their own good.

Always Read the Label

Food labelling is strictly governed by law and manufacturers can't just say what they like on labels. For example, a food can't claim to be 'reduced calorie' unless it is much lower in calories than the usual version.

Highs and lows

When you see health and nutrition claims on food labels you need to view them with caution, as they aren't yet all defined in law. This means that they can mean different things on different food products. The term 'low-fat' is an example of a claim that has been defined. It means the product should contain no more than 3g of fat per 100g. In contrast, claims such as 'helps maintain a healthy heart' have yet to be defined. The Food Standards Agency is working on new rules to ensure that the only claims allowed will be those defined in law. This will make it easier for people to trust the sorts of claims we see on food labels. In the meantime, you will need to try to check the claims yourself by looking at the nutrition panel and by checking the ingredients list.

Pictures

The pictures on packets and labels must not be misleading. A raspberry yoghurt that gets its flavour from artificial flavouring, and not from fruit, is not allowed to have a picture of raspberries on the pot.

Descriptions

It's illegal for labels to have false information or misleading descriptions, but a few well-known foods are allowed to keep their names because we know what they are. We know, for example, that Swiss rolls don't have to come from Switzerland or Yorkshire puddings from Yorkshire, and cream crackers don't have to contain cream. But if something we expect to come from a specific place – such as Cornish clotted cream – isn't made there, the label must say where it's made.

Advice on labels

It's important to pay particular attention to:

- date instructions, such as 'use by' and 'best before' – to avoid or reduce the risk of food poisoning
- defrosting and cooking times – to make sure that any harmful bugs are killed
- storage instructions and directions for preparing food – because correct handling can protect us against food poisoning

But you don't need to worry if the 'display until' date has been reached. This is an instruction to shop staff. Just check the 'use by' or 'best before' dates instead.

And remember, don't eat or cook anything you're not sure about. If in doubt – throw it out.

Source: The Food Standards Agency.
For more information on labelling visit their web site www.food.gov.uk

Arrow Farm Shop

Arrow Farm Shop is located at the border of three counties: Derbyshire, Nottinghamshire and South Yorkshire. This excellent location allows a wide range of locally sourced produce.

The shop is run by the Blagg family, who have had over fifty years of farming experience. The farm has been selling home grown potatoes to the general public for many years. As a result of a steady increase in farm gate sales it became apparent that there was an opening in the market for fresh quality produce, so in 1991 they converted a disused farm building to establish the farm shop. Their aim is to source direct from the farm, neighbouring farmers and local producers, although naturally there are some items which have to come from further afield. These items are carefully selected and, wherever possible, bought direct from the producers.

Almost all of the potatoes sold through the shop are grown and packed right there at Arrow Farm. The predominantly limestone-based soil is suitable for growing many varieties, the most popular being the Marfona. The Marfona potato has a light yellow skin and yellow flesh with a smooth waxy texture, making it ideal for all cooking methods. The potatoes are packed into bags of various sizes ranging from 2 – 20 kg for your convenience.

The shop offers a wide variety of fresh fruit and vegetables. There is an excellent display of preserves, pickles, cakes and hand-baked biscuits, along with free range and farm fresh eggs. Complementing this is a full range of apple juices, fruit cordials and flavoured water.

The butchery counter is known for its friendly personal service. Master butchers are on hand to offer any help and advice in the choice of cuts of meat required. The beef is reared on their own farm and is hung for fourteen days to ensure that the flavour and tenderness are at their best. The lamb is reared by local farmers who produce to the highest standard and quality, once again ensuring flavour and taste. The pork sold comes from a renowned local pig farmer in Wellow, Nottinghamshire. The pigs are born and reared in an outdoor pig unit which is farm assured with full traceability.

Sausages are sold in a range of flavours from traditional pork to their speciality beef and Guinness, which are made at the shop along with beef, lamb and pork burgers. At the recent National Sausage Awards, held at the Foodex Meatex Exhibition at the NEC in Birmingham, Arrow Farm Shop was delighted to be awarded a Bronze Certificate for their traditional handmade pork sausages and a Silver Certificate for their speciality beef and Guinness sausages.

More recently a delicatessen department was opened, which showcases a range of the finest locally sourced cheeses, succulent fresh cold meats and a selection of Continental delicacies.

The shop is open seven days a week with ample free parking available. For further information please contact the shop on 01909 723018 or alternatively visit their website at www.arrowfarmshop.co.uk.

Scottish Malt

The Classic Malts of Scotland – A Personal View

Until the 1960s single malt was never marketed in a big way; it was considered that delicate non–Scots (palates that is) only liked the easyidrinking, lighter blended whiskies such as Haig, Bells and Grouse. Then some companies started to mass-market some of the lighter malts.

By the mid 1980s the mighty Distillers Company had decided to bring out their own range, but they were not just sticking to the easy drinking styles; they wanted to show the vast range of flavours. They opted to show the different characteristics associated with different areas of Scotland, and they came up with The Classic Malts of Scotland range – six expressions from the Lowland, Speyside, Highland, West Highland, Islands and Islay regions. It was quite revolutionary at the time, and something only a large company with many distilleries could do. The distilleries are:

Lowland – Glenkinchie, 12 years old
Known as the Edinburgh malt because the distillery is near the capital. A few years ago at a prestigious whisky dinner my wife Alison and I were lucky enough to meet the Princess Royal, who is a delightful and interesting lady, taller than I expected with a good firm handshake – after all, she is a horsewoman. As

Lagavulin lyne arm

in Derbyshire

is usual when mixing with the Royal Family there was a lot of waiting around, so when we eventually got to our tables we were ready for a dram. The Glenkinchie waiting for us was light, delicate and flowery, a typical lowland whisky which fits with the gentle rolling countryside the distillery is set in, and just what we needed as an aperitif.

West Highland – Oban, 14 years old
If we head north west from Glenkinchie and Edinburgh, we come to the gateway to the isles – the town of Oban. This distillery is right in the middle of the town just a few yards away from the quayside. The area is rugged and challenging as the majestic mountains sweep down to the sea. I discovered this whisky back in the early 1990s when I was still young enough to think that camping was fun. The weather was typical of the western Highlands, cold and wet – serves us right for going in August. The Oban distillery tour was therefore a must, not least for the free dram at the end. It was a perfect restorative. The colour is an inviting amber, the nose is of smoky heather, the palate has plenty of flavour and body, with honey-rich fruit and a slight smokiness, and the finish is long and dry. Very much the whisky you want after a day in the surrounding countryside.

Highland – Dalwhinnie, 15 years old
We now turn north east and up into the Grampian mountains. At 1073 feet above sea level, Dalwhinnie is the highest of Scotland's distilleries; in fact, the settlement is officially the coldest place in the British Isles with an average temperature of 6 degrees centigrade. The name means meeting place, and in days gone by when the great herds of black cattle were driven down out of the Highlands and Islands to market in Falkirk, herds from north, west and east would meet here. Later the railway stopped here, and now it is near the

Lagavulin stills

junction of the A9 and A86. During the winter months it is a bleak place, but if you go past at the right time of year Dalwhinnie distillery is surrounded by a purple carpet of blooming heather (I've not noticed the wild mountain thyme though). That is why the whisky is heathery. It is also light gold in colour and malty with a gentle rounded oakyness. A great summertime dram.

Speyside – Cragganmore, 12 years old
Continue east following the Spey Valley, and

Lagavulin washbacks

Glenkinchie

we come to Cragganmore distillery. The Speyside region of Scotland is where the vast majority of malt whisky is made. The pure snowmelt water running off the Grampians to the Moray Firth is excellent for making whisky and the ability to see Customs Officers coming through the mountains helps (until 1825 the majority of whisky was made illegally). The whisky from this area was in great demand from the latter part of the nineteenth century from blenders; the whisky got to the blenders via the Strathspey Railway. Cragganmore was built in 1869, but it originally had no road serving it, as all the supplies came in and whisky went out by rail; there is still a picture of a steam train on the box. The whisky is rich complex, and like a heavy fruit cake; it feels heavy on the tongue but slides down well. This is perfect for the heart of any blend, but better on its own.

Island Talisker, 10 years old
The Isle of Skye is beautiful. However, the countryside is untamed, particularly the

Black Cuillin mountains. It is also a timeless place; while visiting the island on a Sunday I was surprised to see all the men going to church in kilts. That just about sums up the whisky; it is also untamed, timeless, and a little old-fashioned some may say. The nose is pungent, the flavours peppery with rich spices. The body is big and syrupy, but the overall effect beautiful.

Islay Lagavulin, 16 years old

It is no accident that I have saved the best till last, and that is not only my opinion. Lagavulin from the island of Islay is the most popular of the classic malts range; in fact at one time sold more than the other five put together. Islay is magical; it gets into the blood and draws you back to it. The whisky is equally magical, the peat smoke is what comes across the most, but there is also a rich earthy quality to Lagavulin. You can almost taste the North Atlantic which sits right outside the distillery doors, and the finish warms you like a roaring peat fire. Just what you need to see off a midwinter storm, or on a summer evening just as it's getting cooler – trust me, I've tried it.

Adrian Murray is a Director and founder of The Wee Dram, an exclusive whisky shop based in Portland Square, Bakewell. For further information please ring 01629 812235.

Dalwhinnie

'"Let your food be your medicine, and your medicine be your food."
– Hippocrates'

Recipes
for Spring

Spring Lamb Casserole

Ingredients
1.2kg boned lamb shoulder, cubed
1 large red onion
10 young spring onions
10 baby leeks
10 baby carrots
Baby shallots
Handful of young peas
2 bay leaves
2 spring of rosemary
Seasoning
300ml dry white wine

Method
1. Heat some oil in a casserole dish.
2. Slice the large red onion into chunky slices, place in the casserole dish and cook until golden. Add the bay leaves and rosemary. Layer the lamb on top and cover with boiling water. Place on the lid and bring to a simmer; leave for 1 hour.
3. Then, in a separate casserole dish place the sliced vegetables. Strain the lamb (retaining the liquid) and add to the vegetables. Add the liquid now with all the flavours of the lamb and onion, to the vegetable casserole.
4. Add the dry white wine and season to taste.
5. Cover and cook for a further 10 minutes.
6. Add the peas and cook for a further 10 minutes.

Smoked Chicken Mousse with Goats' Cheese

Ingredients
200g smoked chicken breast, cubed
75ml Italian beer
50ml crème fraiche
2 apples
1 lemon, juiced
Handful of mint leaves
60g soft goats' cheese
Soft brown sugar

Method
1. Preheat the grill.
2. Place the cubed chicken in a liquidizer with the crème fraiche and beer. Mix until soft.
3. Divide into four buttered ramekins.
4. Peel and dice the apple and chop the mint. Sprinkle onto the chicken mousse and drizzle over a little of the lemon juice.
5. Crumble the goats' cheese and place on top of the apple. Sprinkle with some brown sugar and place until the grill until the cheese starts to melt and the sugar goes golden brown.
6. Serve with caper berries pickled in white wine vinegar and a glass of Italian Peroni.

"There is no sight on earth more appealing than the sight of a woman making dinner for someone she loves."
– Thomas Wolfe

Pesto and Fresh Tuna Pasta Salad

Ingredients
225g fresh medium pasta shells
$^1/_3$ cucumber
100g cherry tomatoes
150g fresh tuna fillet
Fresh lemon juice
Olive oil

Method
1. Fill a large saucepan with water. Add a generous pinch of salt and bring to the boil. Add the pasta and cook according to packet instructions.
2. Dice the cucumber into small chunks and halve the cherry tomatoes.
3. Strain the pasta and place in a large bowl. Stir in the pesto.
4. Heat some oil and a knob of butter in a flat-bottomed pan. When the butter has melted add the fillet of tuna, cover with a lid, and gently cook.
5. Gently prise apart the centre of the tuna to check that it is cooked. It should only take a few minutes.
6. Roughly flake the tuna and stir into the pasta, along with the chopped cucumber and tomatoes. Season and add a squeeze of lemon juice and a drizzle of olive oil.

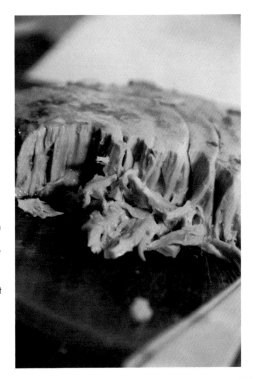

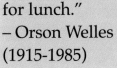

"Ask not what you can do for your country. Ask what's for lunch."
– Orson Welles
(1915-1985)

Marinated Fillet of Beef with Herb Crust

Ingredients
4 fillets of beef
4 tbsp grain musatrd
25g butter
350g spinach leaves
Seasoning

For the sauce:
25g butter
2 tbsp chopped shallots,
1 garlic clove, chopped
150g wild mushrooms, sliced
125ml red wine
Seasoning
125ml beef stock

For the spice rub:
15g ground ginger
15g ground cinnamon
15g ground cumin
15g ground fennel
15g peppercorns

For the crust:
100g breadcrumbs
½ tsp thyme leaves
2 tbsp parsley, finely chopped
25g wild mushrooms, finely chopped
25g spring onions, finely sliced
100g butter
50g Cheddar cheese, grated

Method
1. First make the spice rub. Mix together all the spices, rub over the beef and leave to marinade for 1 hour in the fridge.
2. To make the crust, in a food processor blend together breadcrumbs, thyme and parsley until they are evenly mixed, then add the wild mushrooms and spring onions and blend well. Finally mix in the butter and cheese.
3. Place the crust mixture in foil and roll to make a barrel shape to the size of the beef fillets. Freeze until firm.
4. In a large pan cook the fillet for 3–4 minutes on each side for medium rare, or to your taste. Remove from the heat and leave to rest for 5 minutes.
5. To make the sauce, melt the butter in a hot saucepan and add the shallots and garlic. Fry until softened. Stir in the mushrooms and continue to cook for 4 minutes. Remove from the pan. To the same pan add the red wine and stock and reduce by simmering until thickened.
6. In a separate large saucepan, melt the butter and add the spinach. Wilt down for a few minutes and season.
7. Brush the top of the beef with mustard, then slice the spring onion crust to 1cm thick and place on top of the beef. Place under a hot grill until it starts to melt and turn a golden brown.
8. Serve each beef tournedos on a bed of spinach surrounded by wild mushrooms and pour over the red wine sauce.

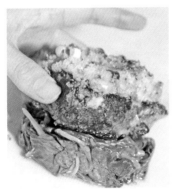

Florentines

Ingredients
75g golden syrup
75g butter
25g plain flour
25g mixed peel with cranberries
50g glace cherries, chopped
50g flaked almonds
1 tsp lemon juice
100g plain chocolate

Method
1. Line two baking sheets with greased greaseproof paper. Place the syrup and butter into a pan and heat until the butter has just melted.
2. Sieve the flour and stir into the butter, with the cranberries, cherries, almonds and lemon juice. Allow the mixture to cool slightly.
3. Pile about 10 spoonfuls of the mixture on each of the baking sheets, allowing plenty of room for the biscuits to spread. Bake at 190°C, 375°F, Gas mark 5 for 15 minutes until golden brown.

Remove from the oven and allow to cool on the sheets for 5 minutes, then place on a wire rack.
4. Break the chocolate into small pieces and put into a basin over a pan of hot water until it has melted. Carefully spread the chocolate over the undersides of the biscuits and make a pattern on it with the prongs of a fork while still soft.
5. Leave to set.

Sea Bass, Asparagus and Seafood Medley

Ingredients
2 sea bass fillets, each 170g
4 fresh basil leaves
1 tbsp olive oil
4 pieces of French stick (cut diagonally)
2 tbsp sun-blushed tomatoes
Basil oil

For the asparagus:
4 spears of large green asparagus, blanched
4 slices smoked salmon, 2 cut into thin strips, the remaining 2 left whole

For the chive oil:
1 tbsp olive oil
½ tbsp chives, chopped
White wine vinegar, to drizzle

For the seafood salsa:
1 small shallot, finely chopped
1 tbsp white wine vinegar
1 tsp sugar
50g mixed seafood medley, washed and chopped

Method
1. Set the oven to 180°C, 350°F, Gas mark 4. Take each sea bass fillet and make a few incisions into the skin. Push some basil into each slit, then drizzle with olive oil.
2. Place the fish in a roasting pan and roast for about 6 minutes. Remove from oven.
3. Take each slice of French stick and top with the sun-blushed tomatoes. Place the sea bass on top. Reserve until ready to serve.
4. Mix the chopped chives and olive oil together. Take each spear of asparagus and roll in the chive oil, add vinegar and season to taste with salt and pepper. Wrap a strip of salmon in a spiral manner around each asparagus spear.
5. To make the seafood salsa, mix together the chopped shallot, vinegar, sugar, chopped seafood, salt and pepper.
6. To serve, reheat the sea bass in the oven for about 3 minutes, until hot and cooked through, and drizzle with basil-infused oil.
7. Arrange the asparagus, salmon and seafood salsa on the plate and serve immediately, with the hot sea bass.

Lemon & Passion Fruit Shortbread

Ingredients

225g unsalted butter, at room temperature
75g caster sugar
275g plain flour, sifted
75g fine semolina
1 tsp grated lemon zest
flesh and seeds from 1 ripe passion fruit
pinch of salt
extra caster sugar, to taste

Method

1. Preheat the oven to 160°C, 325°F, Gas mark 3.
2. In a large bowl, beat together the butter and caster sugar until the mixture turns a lighter colour and is creamy in consistency. This can be done with a wooden spoon rather than an electric mixer. Beat in the flour, salt, semolina, lemon zest and passion fruit, then use your hands to form a pliable dough.
3. On a floured surface, roll your dough with your hands into a long sausage shape, roughly 5cm in diameter. Wrap in cling film and put in the fridge for about 30 minutes.
4. Once chilled, cut 1cm rounds with a sharp knife, trying not to put too much pressure on the dough or you'll end up with a flat edge to the biscuits.
5. Place the rounds on a couple of greased baking sheets and bake in the oven for about 35 minutes until lightly golden. Lift gently from the tray and sprinkle with caster sugar. Once they're cool, enjoy straight away or store in an airtight container.

Pan-Fried Pork Loin

Ingredients

Pork loin, 3 x 50g medallions
½ red pepper, sliced
3 medium mushrooms, sliced
2 tablespoons brandy
1 teaspoon mushroom bouillon
125ml single cream
Seasoning and parsley garnish

Ingredients

1. Pan fry the pork medallions in butter until tender, approximately 8 – 10 minutes.
2. Add the peppers and mushrooms and sauté for 2 minutes.
3. Add salt, pepper and brandy.
4. Add cream and mushroom bouillon and reduce.

Presentation

Place the medallions on your plate, overlapping to add height, nappe the peppers and mushrooms and sauce over the pork.
Garnish with a sprig of fresh parsley.

Prepared by Lon Simpson
at The Denby Lodge, Church Street, Denby Village,
Ripley, Derbyshire DE5 8PH
Tel 01332 881089   www.denbylodge.co.uk

Signature dish

Smoked Haddock & Spring Onion Fishcakes

Served with buttered spinach and a chunky tomato sauce
From the Mainsail Restaurant and Gallery Café
Serves 4

Ingredients

For the fishcakes:

½ diced onion
1 clove garlic, finely chopped
150g smoked haddock
75g white fish (cod or pollock)
1 bunch of spring onions
3 large potatoes – boiled and roughly crushed
Squeeze of lemon juice
Fresh chopped parsley

For the chunky tomato sauce:

1 onion
1 clove garlic
3 tablespoons vinegar
1 tablespoon sugar
Small tin tomatoes
1 tbs tomato puree
Handful of fresh cherry tomatoes
Fresh chopped parsley

Method

For the fishcakes:

1. Pre-heat oven to 180°C, 350°F, Gas mark 4.
2. Sweat off the garlic, onion and spring onion
3. Add the fish and a squeeze of lemon juice and cook for 10 minutes.
4. Bring the potatoes to the boil, cook until tender and crush (season with salt and pepper).
5. After fish and potatoes are cooked drain them both until dry.
6. Bind both together and allow to cool. Check seasoning to taste.
7. Firm into fishcakes when cooled.
8. Dip into flour and then the egg wash, and finally coat with the breadcrumbs.
9. Fry for 2 minutes then place in the oven for 15 minutes.

For the chunky tomato sauce:

1. Sweat off the onions and garlic.
2. Add the vinegar and sugar.
3. Add the tinned tomatoes, tomato puree and cherry tomatoes.
4. Reduce down, season and add the parsley.

For the spinach (optional):

1. Wilt down 2 handfuls of spinach with butter, seasoning and some nutmeg for 1 minute and serve warm.

experience
Carsington Water

The Mainsail Restaurant and Gallery Cafe,
Carsington Water Visitor Centre, Near Ashbourne, Derbyshire DE6 1ST

"My doctor told me to stop having intimate dinners for four. Unless there are three other people."
– Orson Welles (1915-1985)

Recipes
for Summer

Picnic Chicken Wrap

Ingredients
8 chicken breasts
8 small tortilla wraps
8 tbsp guacamole
Mixed lettuce leaves

Marinade:
2 garlic cloves, crushed
Juice of 1 orange
2 tbsp light soy sauce
3 tbsp clear honey
½ tsp fresh mild green and red small chillis, chopped very finely

Method
1. Place the garlic, orange juice, soy sauce, honey and chilli into a bowl. Season to taste and stir.
2. Slice the chicken breasts at an angle into ½ inch wide strips. Place in a large shallow roasting tin, pour over the marinade and turn the strips of chicken breasts over to coat all sides. Cover with foil or cling film and chill in the fridge to marinate for at least 1 hour.
3. Preheat the oven to 220C/425F/Gas mark 7. Remove the foil or cling film from the roasting tin and turn the chicken in the honey marinade once more.
4. Place the roasting tin in the oven and cook the chicken for 25–30 minutes, turning every 10 minutes through cooking and basting with the glaze. Cook until the chicken is tender and slightly blackened.

5. Remove from the roasting tin and leave to cool on a plate. Once cooled, slice the chicken into bite-sized pieces.
6. Lay a tortilla on a board. Place a spoonful of guacamole onto the centre and spread out a little. Add a handful of the mixed lettuce leaves and top with several strips of chicken.
7. Fold the tortilla over the filling, leaving the chicken slightly sticking out. Fold a paper napkin around the tortilla to keep it secure; this will also make it easier to eat on a picnic.

Sea Bass
with Green Pea Veloute

Ingredients
2 sea bass fillets
1 red onion, sliced
4 young carrots, sliced
½ bulb fennel, sliced
500g fresh petit pois
4 tbsp double cream
300ml cider
Seasoning

Method
1. Heat some oil in a flameproof casserole dish and add the sliced vegetables. Stir and cook until tender and glazed.
2. Add the cider and bring to a simmer. Add the peas and cook for a further 5 minutes until all the vegetables are cooked.
3. In a separate frying pan heat some oil and a knob of butter. Add the sea bass fillets and cook until lightly browned, turning once carefully.
4. Place the vegetables in a food processor and blitz until they have formed a thick vegetable purée.
5. Pour into soup dishes, spoon a drizzle of the cream on top and carefully place on the sea bass. Serve with a sprig of mint.

"Work is the curse of the drinking classes."
– Oscar Wilde (1854-1900)

Steamed Mussels

Ingredients
800g mussels
40g green pesto
200ml rosé wine
2 celery sticks
2 leeks
1 onion
2 cloves of garlic
Handful of chopped parsley
Handful of chopped basil
Seasoning

Method
1. Wash the mussels in cold water.
2. Chop all the vegetables and herbs and mix together with the pesto.
3. Lay a large sheet of foil on a work surface, layer another sheet of foil over to make a cross shape. Place the vegetables in the centre and place the mussels on top.
4. Fold all the foil edges together to make a parcel leaving a gap at the top. Pour in the wine and season. Fold over the gap at the top and place on a baking sheet, ensuring there are no gaps in the foil.
5. Bake at 200°C/400°F/Gas mark 6 for 25 minutes.
6. Serve by placing the foil parcel on a warm plate, scoring a cross in the centre and pulling back the corner. Serve with chunks of fresh white bread.

"Part of the secret of success in life is to eat what you like and let the food fight it out inside."
– Mark Twain

Scotch Eggs

Ingredients
4 large eggs
2 tbsp fresh parsley
450g sausagemeat
2 tbsp plain flour, seasoned
1 egg, beaten
100g dry white breadcrumbs
sunflower oil for frying

Method
1. Boil the eggs for 10 minutes, until hard. Rinse under cold water and peel off the shells. Rinse and dry well.
2. Chop the parsley up quite fine and mix well into the sausagemeat, with salt and pepper to taste.
3. Divide the sausagemeat mixture up into 4 equal portions.
4. Take a large piece of cling film and lay it flat on a work surface. Place 1 portion of the sausage mixture in the middle of the cling film, place another piece of cling film on top, and with a rolling pin roll the meat so that it makes a circle large enough for an egg to sit in the middle and the meat to be folded around it.
5. Roll a dry egg in the seasoned flour and place in the middle of the meat. Using the cling film bring the sausagemeat gently around the egg to the middle. Cup into your hands to ensure the meat is sealed together evenly, with no gaps.
6. Repeat with the remaining eggs.
7. In one bowl place the seasoned flour. In another bowl beat an egg, and in a third bowl place the breadcrumbs.
8. Heat a good 4cm depth of oil in a saucepan until it's hot enough to brown a cube of bread in 1 minute.
9. Now roll your sausage-covered eggs one by one in the flour, then dip in egg, and finally coat evenly in breadcrumbs.
10. Fry 2 eggs at a time for 8–10 minutes, until golden brown. Place on kitchen paper to remove any excess oil and allow to cool.
11. Keep refrigerated.

Cherry Trifle

Ingredients
350g plain sponge
1 large egg, separated
4 tbsp caster sugar
250g Mascarpone cheese
A few drops of vanilla extract
250ml whipping cream
475g fresh cherries
4 tbsp water

Method
1. Wash the cherries and de-stone them, and place in a saucepan with the water and half of the caster sugar. Allow to simmer for 10 minutes until they are starting to burst, then remove from the heat.
2. In a large serving bowl, break up the sponge and push to the bottom of the dish. Pour over the warm cherries and juice, leave to cool and allow the sponge to soak up the cherry juice.
3. Whisk together the egg yolk and the remaining caster sugar until pale. Mix in the Mascarpone and vanilla.
4. Whip the cream until thick and fold into the Mascarpone mixture.
5. In a dry clean bowl, whisk the egg white until almost stiff and fold this into the Mascarpone mixture.
6. Pour over the sponge and cherries and allow to cool in the fridge for at least 1 hour before serving.
7. Decorate with a few fresh blackcurrants.

Rhubarb Tart with Southern Comfort Whiskey and Ginger

Ingredients

For the tart:
500g sweet pastry, rolled out to 5mm thickness
1kg rhubarb, cut into 5cm lengths
3–4 tbsp caster sugar
4 tbsp Southern Comfort
6 pieces stem ginger, finely chopped

For the custard:
150ml single cream
150ml whole milk
5 free-range egg yolks
1 tsp cornflour
75g caster sugar

For the crumble topping:
75g butter
200g Scottish shortbread, crumbled

Method

1. Preheat the oven to 180°C, 365°F, Gas mark 4.
2. Place the rolled-out pastry into a deep loose-bottomed 10 inch tin and press the pastry into the sides. Place into the fridge to chill for 30 minutes, then remove and line the pastry case with baking parchment. Fill the case with baking beans and place onto a baking sheet.
3. Place into the oven to bake blind for 15 minutes, then remove the baking beans and baking parchment and return the tart case to the oven. Bake for a further 10–12 minutes, or until golden-brown and cooked.
4. Meanwhile, place the rhubarb onto a baking tray and cover with the sugar to taste, Southern Comfort and ginger. Transfer to the oven to roast for 15 minutes, or until the rhubarb is tender.
5. For the custard, place the single cream and milk into a pan and bring nearly to the boil.
6. Place the egg yolks and sugar

into a bowl and whisk to combine.
7. Pour the hot milk and cream mixture over the eggs mixture and whisk well to combine.
8. Return the custard to the pan over a low heat and bring to a gentle simmer, stirring constantly, until the custard has thickened. Add 1 tsp cornflour if the custard is not thick enough.
9. For the crumble topping, place the butter and crumbled Scottish shortbread in a bowl and mix to form a breadcrumb-like mixture.
10. Pour the crumble mixture onto a baking tray and place into the oven to bake for 15 minutes, or until golden brown. Remove from the oven and stir the crumble topping to break it up into pieces.
11. To assemble the crumble, place three quarters of the rhubarb into the tart case, packing the rhubarb as densely as possible.
12. Pour the custard over the top, then transfer to the oven to bake for 15 minutes, or until the custard has just set.
13. Remove from the oven and sprinkle the custard with the crumble topping.
14. Place the remaining rhubarb into a small food processor and blend to a purée.
15. To serve, place a slice of tart onto each plate and serve with a spoonful of the rhubarb purée alongside.

Mars Bar Cheesecake

Ingredients

Base:
300g crushed digestive biscuits
175g melted butter/margarine

Topping:
300ml double cream (whipped)
500g cream cheese
110g caster sugar
5 sheets of gelatine
3 Mars Bars
A little boiling water
Small quantity melted chocolate

Method

Base:
1. Grease a round tin with a removable base, lining the base with foil or greaseproof paper.
2. Mix the melted butter and crushed digestive biscuits together.
3. Flatten into bottom of tin and refrigerate.

Topping:
1. Place gelatine in a bowl with boiling water and leave for 5 minutes.
2. Whisk cream cheese and caster sugar together.
3. Microwave gelatine and water for 30 seconds or until completely melted.
4. Add to cream cheese mixture and mix well.
5. Add the whipped cream and chopped up Mars Bars.
6. Pour onto biscuit base and leave to set.
7. Once set, drizzle with melted chocolate.

Recipe courtesy of
Chevin Coffee Shop
De Bradelei
Belper, Derbyshire

DE BRADELEI STORES

Bourne's Homity Pie

makes 4

cupboard, use in different recipes and notice the difference in the taste!

Mix the ingredients for the pastry and roll out, then place in the dishes. Heat the oil in a pan and add the chopped onions and crushed garlic. Gently sauté until the onions are translucent. Add the cooked onions to the diced potatoes. Add seasoning, chopped parsley, some B's seasoning and three quarters of the grated cheese. Gently fold all the mixture together.

Divide the mixture into 4 and place into the ready and waiting pastry cases (add a little at a time and build up to make a dome shape. At the restaurant we say the shape of St Paul's Cathedral!). With the remaining cheese, sprinkle on top of the newly created homity. Pop in the oven and cook until golden (about 25 minutes) then … abracadabra … enjoy!

Bourne's Restraurant
at Denby Pottery Visitor Centre, Derby Road (B6179), Denby, Derbyshire DE5 8NX
Call: 01773 740799
www.denbyvisitorcentre.co.uk

Filling:
6 cold jacket potatoes, peeled and diced to about 2cm
1 large chopped onion
1 large clove of garlic, crushed
1 tsp chopped parsley
110g mature Cheddar cheese, grated
1 teaspoon olive oil
B's seasoning (see below)

Pastry:
200g wholemeal flour
110g margarine
75ml cold water

B's seasoning:
½ tbsp vegetable oil
2 tbsp each sea salt &

coarse-ground black pepper
1 tbsp poppy seeds
2 tsp celery seeds
1 tsp mustard seeds

Makes 4 x 20cm round individual dishes (lined with greaseproof paper)

Pre-heat the oven to 200°C, 400°F, Gas mark 6

To make B's seasoning, heat everything in a pan over a low heat for about 10 minutes, then allow to cool before putting in an airtight jar. You will have lots left over from this recipe, but keep it in your

"Reminds me of my safari in Africa. Somebody forgot the corkscrew and for several days we had to live on nothing but food and water."
– W. C. Fields (1880-1946)

Recipes
for Autumn

Cheese and Rocket Soufflé

Ingredients
4 free-range eggs, separated
75g Cheddar cheese, grated
3 tbsp single cream
Handful rocket, chopped
½ tsp cornflour
Salt and freshly ground black pepper
2 tbsp chopped chives, plus extra to garnish
2 tsp butter

Method
1. Preheat the oven and a baking sheet to 200°C, 400°F, Gas mark 6.
2. Place the egg yolks, cheese, cream, rocket and cornflour into a bowl and mix together.
3. Place the egg whites in a clean bowl and whisk, until the egg whites form stiff, glossy peaks when the whisk is removed.
4. Fold the egg white mixture into the egg yolk mixture and season well with salt and freshly ground black pepper.
5. Fold two tablespoons of the chopped chives into the egg mixture.
6. Heat the olive oil in a griddle pan, grease four rings and place on the griddle. Pour in the mixture and cook until the tops of the soufflés are just setting.
7. Place in a preheated oven and cook for 5–10 minutes until the top sets and turns golden in colour.
8. Serve garnished with remaining chopped chives.

"Do not offer a person the chair from which you have risen, unless there be no other in the room."
– Hints on Etiquette 1856

Aubergine and Tomato Gratin

Ingredients
1 medium aubergine
Olive oil
1 clove crushed garlic
6 large tomatoes
250g tub humous

For the sauce:
300ml milk
1 tbsp cornflour
Knob of butter
Salt and pepper to taste
1 bay leaf
100g Cheddar cheese
Parmesan cheese

Method
1. Cut a medium aubergine into 1cm thick slices and arrange in a single layer on a large foil-lined baking sheet or grill rack. Brush with 2 tsp olive oil mixed with the garlic. Season lightly and grill for 8 minutes until light golden.
2. Thickly slice the tomatoes and add to the baking sheet, turning the aubergine slices and arranging them over the tomatoes. Brush with another 2 tbsp olive oil. Grill for a further 8 minutes until tender.
3. Arrange some aubergine slices in a shallow heatproof dish and dot with the humous.
4. Arrange a layer of tomato slices on top, then continue layering alternately with aubergine and tomato.
5. In a saucepan, heat the milk. Mix the cornflour with a small amount of cold milk and add the warmed milk. Return to the pan and stir until thickened, then add the butter and Cheddar cheese.
6. Pour over the tomato and aubergine. Sprinkle over the Parmesan cheese and bake at 180°C/350°F/Gas mark 4 for 25 minutes. Serve with a herb salad and warmed olive ciabatta.

Olive, Pepper and Red Pesto Quiche

Ingredients
175g plain flour
85g butter, cut into cubes
Or a packet of ready-made
shortcrust pastry

For the filling:
2 tbsp olive oil
3 shallots, finely chopped
1 red pepper, de-seeded and diced
1 yellow pepper, de-seeded and
diced
4 eggs
1 jar red pesto
142ml carton single cream
100g Gruyère or mature Cheddar
cheese, grated
100g black olives, pitted

Method
1. Preheat the oven to
200°C/400°F/Gas mark 6.
2. In a food processor, blitz the
flour and butter for 20 seconds until
the mixture resembles fine
breadcrumbs.
3. Add 2–3 tbsp cold water and
mix until the mixture comes together
to form a dough, then knead the
dough gently by hand until you
have a smooth ball of pastry.
4. Roll out the pastry onto a lightly
floured surface and use to line a
rectangular flan tin.
5. Prick the pastry base with a fork,
then line the pastry case with
greaseproof paper and fill with
baking beans. Bake blind for 15
minutes. Remove the paper and
baking beans and return the pastry
case to the oven for 5 minutes.
6. Reduce the oven to
180°C/350°F/Gas mark 4. Heat
the oil in a frying pan, add the
shallots and peppers and cook over
a low heat for 5 minutes until
softened. Allow to cool while
preparing the remaining
ingredients.
7. Spread the base of the flan with

a thin layer of red pesto sauce,
followed by a layer of peppers and
onions. Place the whole black
olives on top.
8. Beat the eggs and cream in a
bowl and stir in the cheeses.
Season, then spoon this over the
olives and vegetables.
9. Bake for 30–35 minutes, until
the filling is just set to the touch.
Allow to cool slightly, then remove
from the tin.

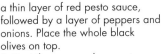

Roast Pork and Roasted Stuffed Apples with Thyme and Parsley

Ingredients

2kg loin of pork, chined (backbone removed) with the rind scored
1 small onion, halved
1 tbsp crushed sea salt
1 tbsp plain flour
300ml dry cider
300ml vegetable stock
Salt and freshly milled black pepper

For the stuffed apples:
400g good quality sausagemeat
8 small Granny Smith apples
2 tsp chopped fresh rosemary
4 finely chopped shallots
Little melted butter
Salt and freshly milled black pepper

Method

1. Preheat the oven to 240°C, 475°F, Gas mark 9.

2. Using a very sharp knife, score the skin of the pork, bringing the blade of the knife about halfway through the fat beneath the skin or ask your butcher to prepare this for you.

3. Using a roasting tin (not too deep as this creates too much steam; make sure the rind of the pork sits above the sides of the tin), put the pork and onion halves in the tin. The onions will caramelize and give a nice flavour to the gravy.

4. Take a spoonful of the sea salt and sprinkle it evenly over the skin, pressing it firmly into the meat. Place the pork on a middle shelf in the oven and roast it for 20 minutes. Turn the heat down to 190°C, 375°F, Gas mark 5 and cook the pork for a further 2 ½ hours.

Continued on page 107

"The only man who is really free is the one who can turn down an invitation to dinner without giving an excuse."
– Jules Renard (1864-1910)

5. Half an hour before the end of cooking time of the pork, prepare the stuffed apples. In a small basin mix the sausagemeat, chopped rosemary and shallots and add a good seasoning of salt and pepper. Remove the core from the apples, then cut a little more out of the apples with a sharp knife to make the cavity slightly larger. Divide the sausagemeat into 8 and roll each piece into a shape that will fit the cavities in the apples. Make a small incision around the outer circumference of the apples. Brush each one with melted butter and insert a little sprig of rosemary on top. Place the apples on a baking tray.

6. Insert a skewer into the thickest part of the meat; if it is cooked the juices that run out should be absolutely clear without any trace of pinkness. When the pork is cooked, remove it from the oven and put the apples in to roast for about 25 minutes.

7. Remove the pork to a warm plate, cover with 2 layers of foil and leave the pork for 30 minutes to rest before carving. Spoon out all the fat from the bottom of the tin, leaving only the juices. Leaving the onion in the tin, place the tin on a low heat on the hob. Sprinkle in the flour and quickly work it into the juices with a wooden spoon.

8. Turn the heat to medium and gradually add the cider and the stock using a balloon whisk, until the gravy starts to simmer. You will have a smooth rich gravy. Discard the onion, season with salt and pepper and pour into a warm serving jug.

9. Serve the pork, carved in to slices; with the gravy and the apples.

Autumn Fruit Crumble

Ingredients
Knob of unsalted butter
2 small Bramley cooking apples, peeled, cored and roughly chopped
2 plums, stones removed and quartered
Small punnet of fresh raspberries
2 tbsp caster sugar

For the crumble:
60g unsalted butter, finely diced
50g caster sugar
1 tbsp luxury muesli
75g plain flour

Method
1. Preheat oven to 180°C, 350°F, Gas mark 4. Melt the butter in a pan, then add the apples and plums. Cook over a high heat for 5–8 minutes until soft and most of the liquid has evaporated. Stir in the raspberries and the sugar. Cook for 2 minutes until the sugar has dissolved, then remove from the heat.
2. To make the crumble, mix all the remaining ingredients in a food processor or rub between your fingers until the mixture resembles breadcrumbs.
3. Divide the fruit mixture between two small ovenproof dishes, about 400ml capacity. Spoon the crumble over the top. Cook for 15-20 minutes until golden brown. Serve with extra thick double cream.

Sparkling Berry Jelly

Ingredients

135g lemon jelly, broken up into cubes
475ml Cava
200g mixed summer berries, such as strawberries, raspberries, blackcurrants and blackberries, hulled and halved if necessary
142ml carton single cream, plus extra to serve
Fresh mint leaves, to decorate

Method

1. Put the jelly cubes in a jug. Pour over 100ml boiling water and stir until the jelly has dissolved. Divide into two jugs, and make the jelly in one jug up to 250ml with the Cava.

2. Divide the fruit between wine glasses, then pour the Cava jelly equally into each, to just cover the fruit. Cover and chill until the surface is just set – this holds the fruit in place, so it doesn't float to the surface.

3. When the second jug of jelly is soft but not set, add the single cream to a level of 250ml and whisk until light and fluffy. (You may need to warm in the microwave to soften the jelly before adding the cream.)

4. Pour onto each jelly and then decorate with whipped cream, fresh mint leaves or fruit when set.

"Preach not to others what they should eat, but eat as becomes you, and be silent."
– Epictetus (55 – 135 AD)

Since taking over The Old Smithy, Beeley, two years ago, Sue and Neil Chatterton have steadily built a reputation for consistently delivering good quality food, aesthetically produced, in the beautiful surroundings of the Chatsworth estate.

They have established many firm "Smithy" favourites, but the most requested is undoubtedly Sue`s Lemon Meringue. Here she dispels the myth that a truly good Lemon Meringue is difficult to make.

The Mythical Meringue

This makes a generous 8 portion flan-dish-sized dessert. Halve the recipe if you want less, but most people will want seconds, and it will keep in the fridge for a few days if not consumed immediately!

Recipe

450g good shortcrust pastry
4 medium unwaxed lemons (zest and juice)
500g caster sugar
8 free range medium eggs
Water (approx. same quantity as lemon juice)
4 tbsp cornflour

Method

1. Preheat the oven to 180°C, 350°F, Gas mark 6.
2. Roll out the pastry to an even thickness of approximately 1cm, making it big enough to overhang the edge of the dish creating a lip to allow for shrinkage. Prick the base with a fork and bake it "blind" for approximately 15 minutes. This will ensure your meringue does not have a soggy bottom. Turn the oven down to 150°C, 300°F, Gas mark 2.
3. Next combine in a heavy-bottomed pan the lemon zest, juice, water, half the sugar, and the egg yolks. Heat gently.
4. Meanwhile, blend the cornflour with a little water and add this to the pan. Stir continually.
5. When the mixture boils and thickens pour into the pastry shell. Trim off the overhanging pastry with a sharp knife.
6. To make the meringue topping whisk the egg whites on high speed until stiff. Steadily add the remaining caster sugar and continue to whisk until very stiff.
7. Spoon the topping over the lemon and spread evenly.
8. Place in the oven for half an hour until risen and lightly browned.
9. Leave to cool and set for a minimum of two hours, and devour at your leisure.

The Old Smithy, Beeley, Derbyshire is open daily from 9am to 5pm except Wednesday.
Booking recommended.
Telephone 01629 734666.

Signature dish

Beef Tagine with Green Olives

Serves 4
Preparation and cooking time 4 hours
¾ kg braising beef
1 teaspoon paprika
1 teaspoon cayenne
1 teaspoon turmeric
1 teaspoon cinnamon
½ teaspoon ground ginger
2 cloves garlic, crushed
4 tablespoons olive oil
2 tablespoons tomato puree
4 shallots, quartered
1 large potato, cut into 1cm cubes

2 large carrots, cut into 1cm cubes
200g can chopped tomatoes
2 tablespoons fresh chopped parsley
Pinch of salt
60g pitted green olives

1. Trim the beef and cut into 2cm pieces. Mix together the five spices with the garlic, two tablespoons of olive oil and the tomato puree. Turn the beef in this mixture and leave, covered, in the refrigerator overnight.
2. Heat the remaining oil in the tagine base. Fry the

shallots, potatoes and carrots until they begin to colour, and then lift out.
3. Fry the marinated beef until sealed on all sides. Return the vegetables with the chopped tomatoes, any remaining marinade, the parsley and a little salt.
4. Cover and cook over a low heat for 3–4 hours, or until the beef is tender.
5. Stir the olives into the dish and allow 15 minutes to heat through.
6. Bon appétit!

Recipe courtesy of Le Creuset.

Le Creuset is available at The Complete Cook Shop, Unit 3, Granby Croft, Matlock Street, Bakewell, Derbyshire DE45 1EE
Telephone 01629 814499
www.bake-well.co.uk

Signature dish

"The way you cut your meat reflects the way you live." – Confucius

Recipes
for Winter

Crumpets

Ingredients
1 tsp sugar
900ml warm milk
2 tsp dried yeast
400g plain flour
1 tsp salt
½ tsp bicarbonate of soda

Makes 15

Method
1. Dissolve the sugar in the milk. Sprinkle over the dried yeast and leave for 10 minutes in a warm place until frothy.
2. Sieve the flour, salt and bicarbonate of soda together into a bowl. Add half of the yeast liquid and beat well. Gradually beat in the remaining liquid to make a thin batter. Beat well, cover the bowl with a damp cloth and leave in a warm place until the batter has doubled in size.
3. Grease a griddle or thick frying pan and several 8cm crumpet rings. Heat the griddle or pan over a high heat. Pour 2 tbsp of the batter into each ring in the pan. Reduce the heat after 4 minutes and cook the crumpets for a further 6 minutes.
4. Remove the rings and turn the crumpets over to cook on the other side for 2–3 minutes.
5. Serve the crumpets hot, toasted on both sides and thickly spread with butter.

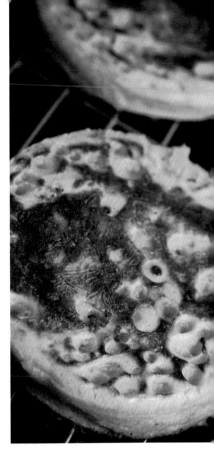

"Never eat more than you can lift."
– Miss Piggy

Leek and Fontina Risotto

Ingredients
300g Arborio rice
5 leeks
Large pat butter, plus a little extra
50g Parmesan
100g Fontina
1 glass red wine

For the stock:
Parsley stalks
1 carrot
2 leeks
1 potato
2 sticks celery
Peppercorns
1 small onion
Bay leaf

Method
1. First make your stock. The exact recipe depends on what is in your cupboard. Don't use too much potato, the stock needs to be very clear.
2. Cook half the leeks in the butter, cooking slowly until they are translucent. Place the other half in a saucepan with a little butter and cook until caramelised. Remove the caramelised leeks and set aside.
3. In the pan with the translucent leeks, turn up the heat and add the rice. Stir for 1 minute for the rice to absorb the flavour, then add half a glass of red wine. Then add the warm stock, bit by bit, until the rice is almost cooked.
4. Add the rest of the wine and the caramelised leeks, reserving some to sprinkle on the top. Keep the heat on until the rice is 'al denté', i.e. not over-cooked, but still with a little bite. Add a small knob of butter and the cheese.
5. To serve, top with the remaining leeks. Serve sprinkled with Parmesan.

Roast Ribs of Traditional Beef with Yorkshire Pudding and Horseradish

Ingredients
2.4kg sirloin of beef on the bone
1 dessert spoon mustard
1 dessert spoon plain flour
4 small onions, peeled and cut in half
Salt and pepper

For the gravy:
25g plain flour
1 litre vegetable stock
Salt and pepper

For the horseradish sauce:
2 tbsp hot horseradish
1 tbsp crème fraiche
Salt and pepper

Method
1. Place the joint on a roasting tin, fat side up. Spread the fat surface of the beef with the mustard and dust with the flour. Season with salt and pepper. Place the cut onion in the roast tin and place the meat on top. The onions will caramelise as the beef cooks and add flavour to the gravy.
2. Cook the beef at 240°C, 475°F, Gas mark 9 for 20 minutes, then turn the temperature to 190°C, 375°F, Gas mark 5 and cook for 15 minutes per 400g for rare. Cook for another 20 minutes for medium, and add an extra 30 minutes of the overall cooking time for well done.
3. Baste during cooking.
4. Remove the beef from the oven, place on a board and leave to stand in a warm place for an hour covered with foil.
5. Place the roasting tray with the

meat juices and caramelised onion on a medium heat. Sprinkle in the flour and using a whisk, blend in the flour using circular movements.
6. Once the mixture becomes a smooth paste, slowly add the stock, continually whisking. Season to taste and allow to continue cooking until slightly reduced to intensify the flavour.
7. Mix together the horseradish, crème fraiche and seasoning. Serve with the beef and gravy.

Taste Tips for Successful Yorkshire Puddings

A basic recipe:
Place in a bowl:
1 medium sized farm egg
1 heaped tablespoon of plain flour
2 tablespoons of milk
and whisk together.
Season to taste.
Add a little more milk until you have the consistency of double cream.
Place the mixture in the refrigerator and allow to rest for half an hour.

Heat the oven to 250°C, 475°F, Gas mark 9.

Using a muffin tin, cover the base of each individual tin with a generous amount of sunflower oil.
Place the muffin tin in the top half of the oven until the oil is extremely hot.
Transfer the mixture into a pouring jug for ease.
Quickly remove the muffin tin from the oven. Pour in the batter and return to the hot oven.
They will take a little over 15 minutes to cook.

Note: This mixture will make three individual puddings. Multiply the ingredients by four to fill a complete muffin tin.

"If more of us valued food and cheer and song above hoarded gold, it would be a merrier world."
– J. R. R. Tolkien

Curried Parsnip and Apple Soup with Parsnip Crisps

Ingredients

400g young parsnips
40g butter
1 tbsp groundnut oil
2 medium onions, chopped
2 cloves garlic, chopped
1.2 litres stock
1 medium Bramley apple
1 heaped tsp coriander seeds
1 heaped tsp cumin seeds
6 whole cardamom pods, seeds only
1 heaped tsp turmeric
1 heaped tsp ground ginger
Salt and freshly milled black pepper

Method

1. In a small frying pan dry roast the coriander, cumin and cardamom seeds. After 2–3 minutes they will change colour and start to jump in the pan. Remove them from the pan and crush in a pestle and mortar.

2. In a large saucepan heat the butter and oil until the butter begins to foam, then add the onions and gently soften for 5 minutes before adding the garlic. Let the garlic cook along with the onions for another 2 minutes, then add all the crushed spices along with the turmeric and ginger. Stir and continue to cook for a few more minutes.

3. Peel and chop the parsnips into 1 inch dice. Add these to the saucepan, stir well then pour in the stock. Season and let the soup simmer as gently as possible for 1 hour without a lid.

4. Slice 1 parsnip thinly and deep fry until golden and crispy.

5. Remove from the heat, then liquidise and sieve. Return to the pan and season.

6. Peel the apple, and as the soup reaches simmering point again grate the apple into it. Serve in hot soup bowls garnished with parsnip crisps.

"Never 'talk at people' it is in the worst possible taste, as it is taking an unfair advantage of them".
– Hints on Etiquette 1856

Chocolate Ricotta Cheesecake

Ingredients

For the base:
50g unblanched whole hazelnuts
175g digestive biscuits
25g dessert cereal
50g butter, melted

For the cheesecake:
150g dark chocolate (70–75 per cent cocoa solids), broken into small pieces
350g Ricotta, at room temperature
200ml half fat crème fraiche, at room temperature
2 large eggs, separated
50g golden caster sugar
3 leaves gelatine
2 tbsp milk

For the chocolate curls:
110g white chocolate (70–75 per cent cocoa solids), broken into small pieces
A little cocoa powder, sifted, for dusting

Method

1. Preheat the oven to 200°C, 400°F, Gas mark 6.

2. Chop the hazelnuts roughly.

3. Place the biscuits in a plastic food bag and crush them using a rolling pin. Then tip the crumbs into a mixing bowl and add the nuts and the dessert cereal.

4. Add the butter to bind it all together, then press the mixture into the base of an 8in spring sponge tin. Pop it into the oven and bake for 10 minutes. Remove it and leave it to cool.

5. Melt the chocolate for the cheesecake in a heatproof bowl over a pan of barely simmering water, making sure the bowl doesn't touch the water, then remove it from the heat and let it cool.

6. In a large bowl, whisk together the Ricotta, crème fraiche, egg yolks and sugar until smooth and well blended.

7. Soak the leaves of gelatine in a small bowl of cold water for about 5 minutes.

8. In a small saucepan heat the milk to a gentle simmer before taking it off the heat. Squeeze the excess water from the gelatine, add it to the milk a leaf at a time, and whisk until it has dissolved. Stir the gelatine and milk, along with the cooled chocolate, into the Ricotta mixture, folding in until it's all thoroughly blended.

9. In a grease-free bowl, whisk the egg whites to the soft peak stage. Then fold a tablespoon of egg white into the cheesecake mixture to loosen it, and then carefully but thoroughly fold in the rest of the egg white. Pour the mixture onto the cheesecake base, cover with clingfilm and chill in the fridge for at least 4 hours, or preferably overnight.

10. To make the chocolate curls, melt the chocolate as before, then pour it onto the base of a plate to form an even layer about ¼in thick. Place the plate in the fridge for 45 minutes to chill and set. Using a large bladed knife or a vegetable peeler, held carefully at either end with both hands, pull the blade across the chocolate, pressing down slightly to form curls. Place the curls in a sealed container in the fridge until you are ready to serve the cheesecake.

11. To unmould the cheesecake, first run a palette knife around the edge of the tin, then release the spring clip and remove it. Carefully lift the cake off the base of the tin and transfer it to a serving plate. Decorate with the chocolate curls and give them a light dusting of sifted cocoa powder.

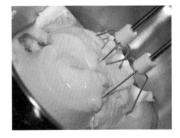

Roast Beef from Arrow farm shop
with Celeriac Mash

Ingredients:
One joint of silverside beef about 1.8 kgs
(Arrow farm sells their own beef and lamb,
assuring you of the finest quality)
2 tablespoons of sunflower oil
Large knob of butter

400g peeled celeriac
600g peeled potatoes (Marfona as grown by
Arrow Farm)
Water

Single cream
Knob of butter.
Salt and pepper

Method:
Pre heat the oven to 190°C, 375°F, Gas mark 5.
Heat the sunflower oil and butter in a large
frying pan until the oil sizzles. Add the joint of
beef and brown on all sides.
Place the beef in a roasting dish, and roast for
17 minutes per 400g for medium rare beef.

In a large saucepan bring to the boil 1.2 litres
of water and add the potatoes and celeriac.
Boil until soft, and then mash the potatoes and
celeriac
adding the cream and butter.
Add salt and pepper to taste.

When the beef has been cooked allow it to
stand for 15 minutes before slicing it and
serving with the celeriac mash.

Honey roast parsnips and carrots make a fine
accompaniment, washed down with a glass of
Brown Cow ale from Bradfield Brewery.

Arrow Farm Shop
Steetley, Worksop, Nottinghamshire
www.arrowfarmshop.co.uk
Tel: 01909 721782

The Bulls Head Repton
Luxury Bread & Butter Pudding

150g sultanas
1 measure of brandy
150g farmhouse loaf
450mlpt double cream
150ml milk
8 egg yolks
150g caster sugar
30g unsalted butter
Pinch of cinnamon
20g of caster sugar for
presentation

Method.
Place sultanas in a saucepan. Cover
with water and brandy. Bring to
the boil.
Remove from heat and allow to
soak for a minimum of 1 hour.

Dice farmhouse loaf into 1cm
cube.s

Custard Mixture.
Whisk together yolks and sugar.
Add milk, cream and cinnamon
Pass through a fine sieve.

Assembly.
Drain off sultanas.
Line each mould with softened
butter.
Layer ingredients – sultanas, bread,
sultanas, bread etc... until moulds
are full.
Place moulds on a baking tray then
fill each one with the custard mix.
Press down on the mixture

ensuring the custard reaches the
base of the mould.
Cook in a water bath (a tray full of
water) in the oven for 1hr 20mins
at 110°C, 225f, Gas mark 3/4

To Serve.
Sprinkle caster sugar on top of
each bread pudding and glaze by
placing under a hot grill (or using a
blow torch.

In the restaurant at The Bulls Head,
High Street, Repton, we serve the
pudding with a crème anglaise and
a toffee sauce.
To book call 01283 704422

signature dish

THE Q BUTCHERS GUIDE
To Cooking Meat

The Guild of Q Butchers provides some interesting guidelines forcooking Sunday lunch or an informal al fresco barbecue. Here are the basic cooking times and tips for beef, lamb, and pork.

FOR BEEF AND LAMB

(credits to EBLEX www.beefyandlamby.co.uk)
There are many delicious ways to cook Quality Standard beef and lamb.

This section gives you great tips on how to prepare beef and lamb successfully, however you choose to cook it.

Meat storage and preparation

Ensure that hands, equipment and surfaces are scrupulously clean before and after handling food and between handling raw and cooked foods,especially when using the barbecue.

Check your fridge is operating at the correct temperature; between 0 and 4 degrees centigrade.

Keep a separate hard, durable chopping board for preparing raw meats.

Defrost frozen foods thoroughly (unless otherwise stated) and do not re-freeze once thawed.

Cover and store raw and cooked foods separately. Store uncooked foods lower in the refrigerator than cooked ones.

Make sure foods are thoroughly and evenly defrosted and when re-heating ensure they are piping hot throughout.

When marinating meat, cover and store in a refrigerator.

Ensure burgers and sausages are thoroughly cooked and piping hot before serving.

When roasting a stuffed joint remember to weigh the joint after stuffing, then calculate the cooking time.

Food thermometers can be used to ensure internal food temperatures are sufficiently hot.

Stir-frying

Stir-frying is an ideal quick method of cooking meat as the thin strips cook in just a few minutes.

It is only necessary to use a very small amount of oil (1 tablespoon) when stir-frying. Use a vegetable-based oil which can be heated to higher temperatures.

Use a non-stick wok or large frying pan. Always ensure that the pan or wok is really hot before adding the meat a little at a time - it should sizzle when the pieces are added.

The meat should ideally be trimmed of excess fat and cut into approximately 1cm strips, cut across the grain to help tenderise the meat and prevent shrinkage.

Method

Heat 15ml (1tbsp) oil in a wok or large frying pan. Add the meat and stir-fry for the recommended time.

Add the hardest vegetables first (e.g carrots, onions) and cook for 2/3 minutes before adding the rest. Add sauce (up to 150ml) and cook for a further couple of minutes.

Guide to roasting

Roasting doesn't need to be complicated. Simply weigh the raw joint and calculate the cooking time using the table below to ensure the meat is cooked to your liking.

Roasting essentials

Position the oven shelves so that the meat is in the centre of the oven.

Place the joint uncovered on a wire rack in a

roasting tin ensuring any fat is on the top. This allows the juices to run down and baste the joint naturally.

When roasting beef and lamb joints, cook them in a moderate oven for slightly longer to ensure even cooking.

Remember to weigh beef and lamb joints before calculating your preferred cooking time.

Allow the joint to rest for 5 to10 minutes after cooking to let the meat fibres relax and juices distribute evenly so the joint is moist and easy to carve.

The degree of cooking can be tested easily using a meat thermometer towards the end of the cooking time: insert into the centre of the joint or at the thickest point, until it reaches the required temperature.

Beef: Rare 60°C, Medium 70°C, Well Done 80°C
Lamb: Medium 70-75°C, Well Done 75-80°C

Roasting in liquid

Slow moist methods include pot roasting, stewing, braising and casseroling. These methods are ideal for tenderising less expensive, less tender cuts of meat and are convenient ways of cooking as they require very little preparation or attention during cooking. Simply pop one in the oven or on the hob and let it cook while you sit and relax.

As it is all cooked in one pot you'll save on washing up too!

Pot roasting

Pot roasting uses whole joints of meat - boned and rolled joints are ideal for pot roasting.

It is traditionally carried out by browning the joint and then cooking in the oven or on the hob with liquid and vegetables.

Allow approximately 450g vegetables (use root vegetables cut into large pieces) and 150ml liquid (try stock, wine, cider, beer etc) for a 1.25kg joint.

Method

Heat 15ml oil in a large heavy-based saucepan or casserole dish. Brown the joint on all sides.

Add the vegetables, liquid and any seasoning or herbs.

Cover and cook either on the hob on a low simmer or in the oven for the calculated cooking time.

Stewing, braising and casseroling

Stews and casseroles use cubed meat, while braising traditionally uses whole steaks or chops.

As with pot roasting the meat is simmered at a low temperature on the hob or in the oven with added liquid.

Allow approximately 225-350g vegetables (use root vegetables cut into chunks) per 450g meat and 150ml liquid (try stock, wine, beer etc).

Method

It is not necessary to pre-seal the meat first; just add all the ingredients to a large pan or casserole dish, cover and cook for the recommended time.

You could also try adding jars of shop-bought sauces to make preparation really quick. This method is ideal for making tasty curries. Simply add a jar of shop-bought curry sauce to some cubed meat and vegetables and cook for the calculated cooking time.

Barbecue tips

Light barbecues well in advance, making sure you use enough charcoal, and wait until it is glowing red (with a powdery grey surface) before starting to cook.

Keep meat refrigerated for as long as possible before cooking.

Make sure the chef doesn't mix up the cooking utensils, boards or plates for raw and cooked meats. Keep them separate.

Always wash hands thoroughly - before preparing food, after touching raw meat and before eating.

Ensure all sausages and burgers are thoroughly cooked before serving (juices should run clear).

Pan-frying

Pan-frying, or 'shallow frying', is a quick cooking method for small, tender cuts using an uncovered pan on the hob.

Use a heavy-based frying pan, sauté pan or wok. For best results, use only a small quantity of oil or butter.

Ensure that the oil is hot before adding your preferred beef or lamb cuts.

Sear each side quickly to seal in juices and retain succulence.

Only turn your steaks once during cooking; leaving them to cook untouched will produce juicier results.

Grilling

A fast, dry alternative to pan-frying for cooking tender cuts, using intense radiant heat either above or below the meat. Char-grilling, or barbecuing, seals the meat juices by forming a crust on the surface of the meat. The meat must be basted with a prepared glaze, butter, oil or reserved marinade mixture. This gives a distinctive flavour to your beef or lamb and keeps the meat moist and succulent.

Only turn your steaks once during cooking; leaving them to cook untouched will produce juicier results.

Under The Heat

Cook the food under a heated element such as a conventional electric or gas grill.

Over The Heat

Brush the meat lightly with oil and ensure that the grill rack is pre-heated. Place the grill rack over a gas or charcoal grill or barbecue.

Between Heat

Place the meat between heated grill bars (such as vertical toaster or grill). This employs radiant heat, convection heat or both.

Baking

This method employs dry cooking in the oven – either in a roasting tin, a sealed container or foil 'packet'. For wonderfully tender meat, choose a clay or terracotta 'brick' which effectively creates a clay oven within your oven. As the oven heats, steam condenses in the pot, basting the meat in its own juices. The end result is moist, tender, full of flavour and naturally cooked with no extra fat.

taste

Dining out Reports

taste dining

Dining at the Coach and Horses has always been a pleasant experience for us at 'taste'. Glen Smith always gives us a cheery smile and our drinks order is quickly taken.

The Coach and Horses
THURGARTON

Looking through the menu we saw that Glen has responded to the economic climate by including food within a lower price range. Intrigued by this move, we perused the menu and chose our starters. The question now was – has the quality suffered? No, is the answer. For one thing it is the same chef, so consistency is maintained and quality ingredients are still evident.

The table setting is highly polished dark oak with silver cutlery and attractive glassware, topped off with fresh flowers and a lit candle. This makes the restaurant look really attractive.

My dining partner chose the pumpkin and coriander soup, which was thick, hot and spicy, spot on for a winter night. My king prawns were the largest I had ever seen, and although they were cooked in garlic, they were very subtle. The prawns were very fleshy and tender, and the pot of mayonnaise and leafy salad were a good accompaniment.

For main course I decided to try the chef's pie of the day, which was pork and ham in cider for just £8.95. This was served in its own dish with a heady crust of puff pastry and a wonderfully varied selection of seasonal vegetables glazed in butter.

Many pies can be very stodgy and heavy going, but this was delicious; the pork and ham were good companions and the sauce was light, slightly sweet and creamy. A generous portion of hand-cut chunky chips completed my meal. My partner chose the Cajun chicken, which was a generous piece cooked on the bone, giving it a superior flavour. It was served with a buttery sweet potato mash and a lime and spring onion crème fraiche, which linked the flavours. He also ordered an extra portion of the home-cooked chips just to test them; he didn't need them but told me that he needed to know about them. Brilliant!

To top it all off, we had a dessert – or, in my language, a pudding! Dark chocolate is known for its digestive properties, and I needed no further excuse to try the dark chocolate terrine. I remembered from before that the chef is famed for his desserts, and he certainly lived up to his reputation. Not sweet, but rich, moist and complemented by an excellent home-made ice cream.

We had our coffee on the settees by the log stove – a very relaxing way to finish our meal. The atmosphere at the Coach and Horses is one I really feel comfortable in; there is plenty of space to sit and relax, the seating is comfortable and you don't feel overwhelmed by the nearness of other customers. It has the friendly feel of a traditional English pub. However, the quality of the food is superb. The chef has an excellent eye for combining good flavours at very reasonable prices.

A great evening with excellent food in warm surroundings.   GP

The Coach & Horses,
Main Street, Thurgarton,
Nottingham NG14 7GY
Telephone: 01636 831311

taste dining

The Sanam Tandoori Restaurant, on King Street, Alfreton, has over the years gained a reputation for consistent food quality, and they plan on staying at the top of their profession by recently completing a total refurbishment of their restaurant and introducing tasty new dishes.

On entering the restaurant you are greeted by a modern style that fits with twenty-first century dining. One thing that hasn't changed is the quality and quantity of the food. The owners are dedicated to ensuring that the food you are served, whether it be in the restaurant or as a takeaway, maintains their exacting high standard.

I am very comfortable with the menu at the Sanam, and have, in recent times become a little boring by 'having the same' each time I visit. This time I asked Iqbal to surprise me. As he knew my taste buds he presented me with Achari Chicken. Quite a change from my normal dish, but absolutely delicious. So change is good!

Their new menu includes the normal firm favourites of Indian

cuisine, but also encompasses new styles and tastes that reflect current dining trends.

On another occasion we were invited to the Sanam to taste some new dishes. The chefs had spent a considerable amount of time to get the blends and tastes of the dishes exactly to their liking. They needed to ensure that once these dishes were on the menu they would be able to prepare them to the same exacting standards that their customers have come to expect. Once this was accomplished they could then present the the new menu to us.

The three new starters we tried included:
Daryayi Nazrana: Fresh salmon, marinated in fresh dill yoghurt and the chef's special spices, roasted in the Tan Dor and served with a delicate mixed fruit chat. This fish starter wowed one of our testers and he doesn't like fish! He actually said he would order it when he came again.

Adraki Lamb Chops: Juicy slices of lamb chop marinated in garlic and spices, cooked in the Tan Dor and served with salad and sauce. The lamb just melted in the mouth and the spices left the tongue feeling quite tingly.

Murg Tikka Hara Bhara: Chicken marinated in ginger, garlic and

The Sanam Tandoori Restaurant

fresh-minted yoghurt with a touch of olive oil, and roasted in the Tan Dor. Served with a special barbecue sauce and salsa. This was the chef's personal favourite.

Paneer Ka Soola: Cottage cheese stuffed with tandoori spices and cooked over charcoal. Ideal not just for vegetarians but for me too. If you haven't tried cottage cheese done this way, you seriously must.

The mains included Chicken Mirch Masala. This is strips of chicken fillet with peppers, onions, tomato, ginger, garlic and chef's special spices for a 'home like' curry. I can't wait to try them, but we must do that another day.

I would highly recommend that you call in and try the new dishes yourself. Bookings are also now being taken for parties.
Call 01773 830690 to book.   GP

taste dining

dining tapas is a time for sharing

Having made extensive travels around Europe, I have found that one of the most exciting ways to eat is tapas. Sitting on the side streets of Ronda, Andalucia just epitomises to me the whole concept of enjoying food in a communal atmosphere while the world wanders by. Tapas is relaxing eating; it is not 'stuffy', and makes those who refuse to share food very cross! Yes, dining tapas is a time for sharing – not only food and wine, but good conversation. When I was asked to visit Iberico World Tapas my heart skipped a beat. Tapas in England – could it possibly match up to my gourmet delights abroad? It is the first time we have reported on a tapas bar, and at the outset I will state that we had a fantastic evening. Here is why.

As you enter the building through the stone arch and drop down the stairs, the room suddenly opens out into a delightful restaurant with a vaulted ceiling. We were greeted by the restaurant manager, who was attentive to our every need throughout the whole evening. If you have eaten tapas-style before then you will know the way the meal goes. If not, don't worry – just tell the waiter the things you like and let them bring you a selection, or you can choose a couple of things per person off the menu to get you started and then keep topping up if you are still hungry as the evening goes on. What could be simpler?

The menu is split into two sections, World Tapas and Spanish Tapas. As we perused the menu we were served sourdough bread with olive oil and balsamic vinegar, just to tickle our taste buds. To start off with we chose a selection of world cheeses and a selection of Spanish meats. The cheese selection included Mahon (chilli tomato jam), Stilton, Murcia al Vino (fig and almond), Morbier, (apricot compote) and Peccorino (truffled honey), all for £7.95. Each came with a small accompaniment, such as finely sliced fennel in a pickle vinegar, which was delicious, and a small slice of almond and fig cake.
The meats were Serrano, Lomo, Salchichon, Chorizo

(of course), and Pata Negra Sorbrasada with truffled honey (my favourite) – again, all for £7.95. Wow, how's that for starters?

The dishes came in steady succession, which is typical tapas style. We went Spanish with the wine and had a bottle of Rioja (£21.00). As we were enjoying these dishes the waiter came and took our next order.

We chose two dishes each from the extensive menu: Seared Venison (£7.50); Corn-fed Chicken (£5.50); Grilled Tiger Prawns (£5.50); and Black Cod in Spicy Miso (£7.50). In addition to this we ordered Spanish Tortilla (£3.50), Patatas Bravas (£3.50), Crispy Courgette Flowers (£6.50) and Padron Peppers (£4.00). Each dish was delicious, but the black cod stood out, wrapped in a leaf. I think it was steamed, and came with a really unusual spicy accompaniment. The crispy courgette flowers were filled with creamy cheese and lightly fried in a tempura batter. Another favourite was the seared venison, which was thinly sliced and pink in the centre. It was tender and had a subtle flavour. The patatas bravas is a traditional Spanish dish, as is the tortilla which is really a Spanish omelette.

Now for the desserts. I would have to say I have always been disappointed with the desserts at tapas bars. They tend to have arrived in a freezer truck, and all restaurants have the same tacky laminated menu. Not so at Iberico; the desserts are carefully thought

out and very individual. The Rhubarb Compote was especially tasty, topped with really creamy rich yoghurt, and then topped again with crunchy ginger biscuits – a winning combination.

The evening was a great success; we all agreed that as a dining experience this was one to savour, and one which would meet with a speedy repeat. Our thanks for making us most welcome and to the staff who described each dish and its flavours as it was served – a real professional touch.

Please note: It is vital that you book a table at Iberico as it is an extremely popular place to dine.

Archie's

The Barn • 4 Bridge Street Sandiacre •
Nottinghamshire NG10 5QT 0115 949 9324

When Archie's restaurant opened in 2006 we were privileged to be among the first to enjoy their particular style of English food, and we were pleasantly surprised by their chef's ability to cook traditional dishes and then give them a twist. Three years later that same ethic and quality are both still in place.

On our arrival we were greeted by owner Paul Rowland, who is very 'down to earth'; chatting to him was most enjoyable, and it was good to see that Archie's Restaurant has maintained its crisp, clean and bright aspect. Archie's is a beautiful old building sympathetically restored in a contemporary style. Warm exposed brickwork, wood floors and wrought ironwork link the two floors with a double height bar, and outside balcony area for use in warmer weather.

The tables have plenty of space to dine at, and there is plenty of walking room between tables. You can dine either downstairs or upstairs, both areas being light and airy.

As we sat with our G & Ts we perused the menu. It's not a cluttered confusing menu – it's straightforward and simple with enough dishes to please most palates. I am very suspicious of massive menus because it's impossible to freshly prepare unless you have oodles of chefs in the kitchen.

The wine menu showed a great variation, each country being well represented. I normally choose a bottle of Rioja as I enjoy its smooth fruitiness but we were dining with family who live in Spain, so that would have been a bit like giving ice to Eskimos. Instead I went for a bottle of Claret which had quite a good aftertaste. I scored well there and have added it to my list of 'wines to drink whilst dining'.

A platter of fresh, warm, home-made bread with chilled butter helped to get us into the dining mood. The ambience in the restaurant was lovely as a steady hum of diners chatted away and relaxed.

As a starter I went for the warmed smoked salmon, which arrived piled high on a bed of crunchy, finely sliced Chinese leaves with pieces of mango and kiwi fruit. Warmed salmon proved a change on a winter evening and the clean taste of the fruit complemented this, the Angostura Bitters dressing contrasting with the sweet fruits.

The char-grilled Porterhouse steak was accompanied by a large field mushroom with half a tomato inside, a stack of hand-made fat cut chips, home-made tomato ketchup dip, and a pot of herb mayonnaise. The flavour of the steak was beautiful and the accompaniments were prepared with care, which well-satisfied my husband.

For a main course I chose the locally farmed fillet of beef. This was served on a bed of leeks with a subtle flavour of tarragon; the char-grilled beef was just right and suited my appetite well, topped with two hand-made ravioli which were filled with Ricotta and tiny cubes of ham and finely chopped herbs, which were surrounded by a dark port gravy. I thoroughly enjoyed this – not too many flavours competing, not too dry, not too heavy on the steak and the ravioli were soft and creamy.

We couldn't resist the sticky toffee pudding with freshly made custard. My baked orange cheesecake was extremely smooth, the Cointreau added a depth of flavour and the tangy orange left your palate feeling clean.

Fresh coffees completed our meal, and whilst we were relaxing Paul came and chatted about the way he was directing Archie's. I must say that as he was talking I could see their work ethic will take Archie's even further along the success route, even in economically hard times.

Our thanks to all at Archie's for making us welcome.

taste dining

O-kra, on New Zealand Lane in Duffield, has achieved remarkable success in a very short period of time, and it was easy to see why as we entered the restaurant one sunny evening.

The most popular cuisine in Britain at the moment is Indian. That should not surprise you, as Indian food has the most delightful spices you can find. Many just think of curries when they think of Indian food but that is not the case. True, the restaurant does serve curry, but there are a host of other dishes to try.

The decor at O-kra is very crisp, using modern colours combined with traditional white linen on the tables. It all adds up to a very clean-lined look. Even the floors have a mix of carpet and wood, helping to create a quiet and understated atmosphere. The whole ambience is conducive to fine dining. We were greeted on arrival by owner Sadique, a very polite man with the ability to put you at ease immediately.

As we struggled to make up our minds whether to have Aloo Tikki – shallow fried potato patties stuffed with peas and raisins served on a bed of yoghurt, mint and tamarind sauce – or the Bharwan Khumb Lazeez – whole mushrooms stuffed with Mozzarella cheese and deep fried in golden batter – Sadique came to our rescue and suggested that we let him decide. Once he had our likes and dislikes clearly in mind he disappeared and we waited with bated breath, and a bottle of Rioja, to see what came. Indian music wafted through the restaurant, and soon all the tables were full; the whole ambience was one of chatter and clinking glasses. There was no rush to leave your table to make room for a second sitting, so you could just sit back and relax.

A sample of starters arrived which included chunks of cottage cheese stuffed with mint chutney, coated with creamy marinade and barbecued with onion and peppers. We also sampled chunks of Scottish salmon marinated with coconut and spices, chargilled in the tandoor, and succulent king prawns in a peanut marinade, scented with coriander and chargrilled.

Two main courses arrived, featuring chicken and lamb. The chicken dish (Murg Massalam) was a whole

O-kra RELAXED FINE DINING

roasted chicken breast and minced lamb with a blend of fresh ingredients which will be prepared to your desired strength. It is worth noting at this point that all the food is freshly prepared and not pre-done in large quantities, so whatever your tastes are they can be catered for. The Achari lamb was cooked with fresh tomatoes, onion and a hint of Indian pickles. Apparently this dish is from the Moghal period and a favourite in India, and I can see why; it was so smooth and full of flavour. In comparison the chicken set my tongue alight with its mass of flavours and delicious spices. We accompanied the main courses with a cheese naan.

Kesrai Rasmalai was my choice of dessert, fluffy light sponge patties in a light milk syrup flavoured with saffron and garnished with pistachio nuts. This was a very palate-cleansing dish and an excellent way to finish a meal. My dining partner chose Pistachio Kulfi, a smooth-flavoured Indian ice cream garnished with fresh fruit.

The chefs at O-kra are of the highest calibre, having worked for international restaurants and hotel groups. This has given them vast experience in people's varying palates – especially the English!

O-kra is open Tuesday – Sunday 5.30pm–11pm. To book call 01332 841156 www.okra.org.uk

dining out at
WORLD SERVICE

With awards and accolades being showered upon it, we thought it was time to test out the praise that is currently being heaped upon World Service Restaurant and Lounge Bar, Newdigate House, Castle Gate, Nottingham, 'Best Overall Restaurant' in Nottingham four times in five years. Would it live up to its reputation?

World Service is set in what to me is a particularly lovely part of the city of Nottingham – not far from the Castle, but close to the centre, and surrounded by properties full of character and history. The restaurant itself is situated in a relatively new building, attached to a seventeenth century property that was formerly a Serviceman's Club. They do still meet there in an upper room, but the building in the main is occupied by World Service and boasts not only a restaurant and bar but also individual rooms for private parties. The external walled oriental garden is an ideal place to start your dining experience, with garden lighting and water features to put you in a relaxed mood. The furnishings are from around the globe and feature many hand-made pieces. Sitting looking at the facade of the old building, it was not hard to let the mind wander and wonder who had visited here in centuries gone by.

We were invited to sit in the garden and enjoy drinks of our choice and a few nibbles. It was immediately noticeable how professional all the staff were.

The cocktail menu is extensive and creative, and makes in itself fascinating reading. A mix of apple juice, elderflower pressé and a generous amount of ice and mint was just one choice that appealed to me.

If you are currently enjoying New World wines, or have a favourite French wine, I'm sure you will find it here alongside wines and champagnes you may choose

to keep for special occasions. Italian lagers and a variety of beers all make it difficult to fault the selection behind the bar and in the cellar.

The menu offers a balanced choice with plenty for all tastes, as you will see.

The starters included a choice of spinach and watercress soup or tomato and roasted red pepper, served with tiny savoury basil scones (v) for £5.00. There were three fish dishes: salted cod croquette, a half lobster and grilled sea bass. The latter was delicious, piled on top of country vegetables and a square of thinly layered crouton, just enough to awaken your palate without spoiling your main course (£8.75).

Dining with friends, I also had chance to taste the soup, duck and local unpasteurised goats' cheese with courgette fritter and piccalilli (v) at £7.50. The combination of textures with the creamy cheese and crisp vegetables in the tangy pickle worked especially well.

Our evening was off to a fine start.

Roast halibut with Boulangere potatoes (£19.50), pan-fried John Dory with a spinach lasagne (£17.75) and Nottinghamshire pork fillet (£17.50) all made the choice of main course a difficult one. Derbyshire fillet of beef with onion tart tatin, green beans and Madeira sauce (£21.00) and the chicken both looked very tempting as they arrived for our friends.

For main course I veered away from my usual steak, and chose the halibut. The first mouthful gave me quite a shock. I had obviously not read the menu properly, and was surprised to bite into peppers carefully hidden in the red onion! However, it was delicious. I particularly enjoyed the bold combination of flavours and textures which livened the usually gentle taste of halibut.

My partner went for the assiette of lamb, which traditionally comes quite rare. The pink centre and richly roasted outside were exceptionally tender and the accompanying sauce made it really moist. Sitting on a bed of smooth creamy potatoes with a golden crisp outer layer, this dish gave a real dining experience. The accompanying vegetables – sugar snap peas and glazed carrots – were crisp and full of taste.

As we sat contemplating the sweet menu the consensus of opinion was to share the assiette of desserts (minimum 2 persons). This gave us the opportunity to taste the whole selection, and from the smooth chocolate and fresh raspberry centre of the warm chocolate bake to the creamy crème brulee and the hot and cold contrast of the baked Alaska and the shot of strawberry essence, the desserts all looked beautiful and tasted divine. We sipped a very light and not too sweet dessert wine before finishing with a cup of coffee, which completed an extremely pleasant and sophisticated dining experience.

We were never short of someone to care for our needs. The staff were not overfussy, but as each course arrived they explained everything on the plate – its content and the flavours. I like that touch; it shows both a knowledge of the menu and a culinary interest which often seems to be missing nowadays. Most places just serve the food and off they go, leaving you asking 'what was that sauce?'

So then, in conclusion, are the awards justified? Well, we would say so, and so would the many other diners in the packed restaurant on that Monday night.

You can book online at www.worldservicerestaurant.com or by phoning 0115 847 5587.

The Saracen's Head Hotel
Southwell

Rack of lamb with champ potato and coconut and mint foam

Since the fourteenth century the Saracen's Head has been serving fine food and, whilst they have kept the traditional interiors of the buildings, the menu has certainly been modernised!

On arrival we were shown to a table in the bar for a drink and to ponder over the menu. The bar area was busy, and if you choose to do so you can dine here from the bar menu. We chose to use the dining area and explore the menu. There are nine main courses and nine starters to choose from, which they add to and swap every few weeks to keep in line with seasonal produce. Once we had chosen our meal they recommended a wine to complement it – this was a Gloriso Crianza Rioja.

We were shown to our table in the dining area which is still very traditional, with oak panelled walls and plush furnishings. The tables were set with crisp white linen and all the tables had fresh flowers. We sat at what we were told was 'illustrious table 15', set in the corner of the room. They explained that people had literally walked out because the table had been booked

before them, so we felt very privileged to be seated there.

For a starter I chose the crispy pancetta and shredded duck salad with a plum dressing. Personally I'm not a big fan of salads as I often find them very bland and quite boring, but this was anything but bland! It was crisp and had a lovely plum dressing, and there was also plenty of shredded duck and croutons. My partner chose a soft poached egg on pan–fried wild mushrooms and nappe of hollandaise sauce. The egg was warm and slightly runny on top of a variety of wild mushrooms and dressed in a light hollandaise sauce.

Table 15

For my main course I ordered pan-seared chicken breast with a potato confit served with a tomato and rhubarb compote. This came on a piping hot plate with a side order of potatoes, broccoli, carrots and beans to share. The chicken was incredibly tender and had a beautiful tomato vegetable compote poured over it. The portions would fill even those with a big appetite! My partner ordered the rack of lamb, which he ordered medium rare, with champ potato and coconut and mint foam. The lamb had a slight hint of mint and the overall texture was succulent and tender. The subtle

hints of coconut gave a vibrant and different taste to the dish.

For dessert we ordered the cheese board. This came with a variety of crackers, Brie, mild Cheddar and Stilton. Unlike most establishments this cheese board came with enough cheese to fill the crackers; the balance was spot on. We also had a chocolate gateau, and as I am a chocolate lover this was perfect for me! Only those with a hearty appetite for chocolate should attempt this as it is a very generous portion. After this I would recommend you retire to the evening lounge, which has nice comfy leather seats and is candlelit – a perfect place to sit back and enjoy a coffee or digestif to finish the evening. *Charlotte*

The Saracen's Head Hotel, Market Place, Southwell NG25 0HE 01636 812701 www.saracensheadhotel.net

taste dining

A typical Derbyshire stone village, Cromford owes much to Richard Arkwright and its industrial heritage. Workers at his mills needed housing, and to support their needs the village grew to include shops such as butchers, haberdashers, saddlers and bakers. One shop in particular, the village bakery, was a popular place until it closed in 2006. After some renovation the building next to the bakery (and originally the baker's living quarters) was opened last summer as a coffee shop and restaurant. Here during the day you can sit on the cobbled forecourt and watch the world pass by, or if the weather is a little inclement, enjoy the cosy interior, where in the evening mood lighting helps to create a pleasant place to dine.

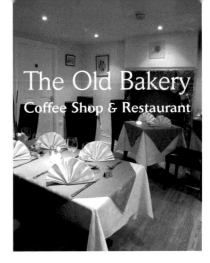

The Old Bakery
Coffee Shop & Restaurant

Owner Simon Smith, along with award winning chef Wayne Ledger, formerly head chef at The Bear, Alderwasley, focuses on providing quality food with locally sourced produce. Light meals and sandwiches are served through the day from a frequently changing menu. Home-made cakes and pastries make this a lovely place to call for a mid-morning coffee or afternoon tea. Our visit, however, was in the evening, and my companion on this occasion was a good friend and also, as it happens, a vegetarian. The Old Bakery frontage belies its interior; decorated in gentle pastel colours, it retains many original features while modern lighting and crisply laundered tableware create a relaxed atmosphere. After a chilled glass of Pinot Grigot we settled down to make our choices.

The à la carte menu gives a choice of four starters, four main courses and three desserts. My choice was the Atlantic Prawn and Melon Cocktail, a good combination of traditional starters, the melon added a freshness which complemented the prawns, and the mayonnaise tied all the flavours together. My friend chose the Baked Egg, served straight from the oven, the yolk nicely runny and with a rich white wine and cream sauce. Sautéed mushrooms and Cheddar added a depth of flavour. Straying from the à la carte menu, I

was tempted by the 'House Special'. The sirloin was well cooked and the sauce- delicious mushrooms and ham in a creamy mustard sauce made it a filling and rich dish. Hand-cut chunky chips and a freshly prepared salad were well chosen accompaniments.

The vegetarian option thankfully wasn't lasagne as it often is, but a flaky filo pastry case filled with a variety of oven-roasted vegetables topped with baked goats cheese. My companion was delighted and really enjoyed this. Chicken Fillet, Derbyshire Lamb, Pork Steak and Baked Halibut were also on the menu that evening, so there was a good balanced choice.

With heart in mouth we both chose the lemon meringue pie for pudding. I must explain that I have never found a lemon meringue to match the one my mother used to make, and have always been disappointed by the artificially coloured, overly sweet and synthetic offerings, so often served. However, this was beautiful, very sharply lemony and not too sweet a meringue - not quite as good as my mother's but very, very near. A good coffee finished a lovely evening off nicely.

The atmosphere here at the Bakery is intimate and relaxed. They produce good quality, freshly prepared food. Jazz nights, game

evenings and tasting evenings are all on the cards, so you need to keep your eye on what is going on here. Owner Simon has many years of experience in the restaurant business and this shows in his ideas and presentation. The wine list includes both European and New World wines. Two course evening meals are from £10, three courses £13.50 and main courses from £7.50. By the way, if you would like to try something a little more unusual, such as camel steak or alligator, give Simon a call and discuss your request with him, and I'm sure he will be able to oblige. The Old Bakery Coffee Shop and Restaurant is at 11-13 Market Place, Cromford DE4 3RE. Open daily from 10am to 8.30pm, and closed on Tuesdays.

taste
Sourcing the Produce

Robin Maycock

HOLLOWAY VILLAGE BUTCHER
Derbyshire's Premier Butchers Shop.

All our meat is selected from Derbyshire and Nottinghamshire farmers by me personally, transported by me and slaughtered in our own licensed premises behind the shop.

HOME-MADE on our premises -
Ham, Ox tongue, Haslet, Roast Pork, Turkey, Salt beef.
Sausages (Fresh daily). Pork and Chive, Pork and Herb, Cumberland, Pork and Tomato, Plain Pork.

HOME COOKED in our own bakery -
Savoury Meat Pies, Quiche, Pork Pies, Scotch Eggs,
Fruit Pies, Cakes and Puddings.

Ready meals.
A selection of meals for every day of the week.
Bring your own dish and let us make a real home-made pie for that special occasion.
Pie and Pea Supper a speciality

English and Continental Cheese. Fresh Fruit and Vegetables.

If you care about food as much as we do
give us a ring on
01629 534333 and ask for Robin or Jonathan.

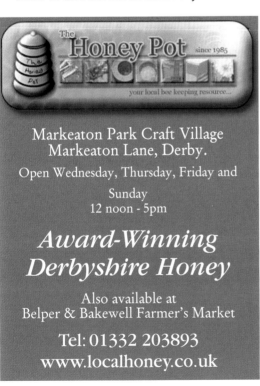

taste
derbyshire & nottinghamshire

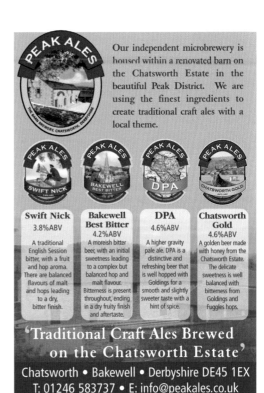

Mr Pitchfork's Pickles

From the Home of Robin Hood

Established in 2002. Award-winning handmade chutneys, pickles and jams all made with quality ingredients.

Buy direct from us or at one of the local shops or farm shops that stock our products. (Visit our website for details)

For all enquiries telephone Bob Pitchfork
0115 9178037 or 07761 428 961
Email robert.pitchfork@ntlworld.com
W39 Nottingham Business Centre, Lenton Boulevard, Nottingham NG7 2BY

taste
derbyshire & nottinghamshire

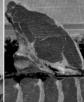

give taste as a gift
buy taste derbyshire
online for only £3.50
and we will post it
FREE of charge*
visit our web site
www.tastederbyshire.co.uk
*UK only

Send cheque payable to
Images Publishing Limited

to Images Publishing Limited
Victoria House, Market Place
Crich, Matlock
Derbyshire DE4 5DD

or phone 01773 850050
(credit and debit cards taken)

or visit our website
www.tastederbyshire.co.uk

taste

Finding Places
to Eat

Take a fresh look at the
Sanam Tandoori Restaurant

Bookings are also now being taken for parties, but don't leave it too long as The Sanam gets booked rapidly. **Call 01773 830690 to book.**

New exciting menu
Newly refurbished restaurant

Same exceptional quality

Take-Away Hotline
FREE delivery on orders over £15.00 within 5 miles radius

01773 830690

The Sanam
Tandoori Restaurant

Authentic Indian food served in a lively
warm and friendly atmosphere

**50 King Street,
Alfreton. Telephone 01773 830690**

Opening Times Sunday to Thursday 6.00pm to 12.00am
Friday & Saturday 6.00pm to 1.00am

taste
derbyshire & nottinghamshire

DE BRADELEI
BELPER
THE SMARTER WAY TO SHOP

Enjoy delicious home cooked food in our

CHEVIN COFFEE SHOP

MASSIVE SAVINGS
Up to 70% discount

WOMENSWEAR • ACCESSORIES • MENSWEAR
SHOES • GIFTS • SOFT FURNISHINGS • LEISUREWEAR

OPENING HOURS Mon-Fri 9.30-5.30 Sat 9.30-6.00 Sun & Bank Holidays 10.30-4.30
FIND US AT Chapel Street, Belper, Derbyshire, DE56 1AR T. 01773 882442
www.debradelei.com

IBéRiCO
WORLD TapaS

Iberico world tapas brings together the rustic simplicity of Spanish tapas together with the refined ingredients of world cooking all presented to you in a stylish and intimate vaulted restaurant.

Located in the heart of the Nottingham's Lace Market, in the historic Galleries of Justice, the grade II listed building offers a great relaxed dining atmosphere with a cosmopolitan interior.

Sit back and relax on soft leather seating with chocolate and cream tones complimented by colourful Moorish tiles and mirror backed frescos.

Iberico is brought to you by the team behind the award winning World Service Restaurant, offering a dining experience of the same quality in a more laid back style.

0115 9410410

OPENING TIMES

LUNCH - Tuesday - Saturday 12noon till 2.00pm
DINNER - Tuesday - Saturday 6.00pm till 10.00pm

The Shire Hall   High Pavement   Lace Market   Nottingham   NG1 1HN
E-mail: info@ibericotapas.com   www.ibericotapas.com

taste
derbyshire & nottinghamshire

Sometimes it's hard to choose the right quality restaurant

Cooking quality food calls for clear thinking, proven expertise and long standing experience.

We aim to build long term relationships with our diners by listening and learning about your specific requirements and offering advice on our limited range exclusive menu.

Each dish is individually hand crafted and freshly made.

Authentic Indian Cuisine
Open Tues - Sunday 5.30 - 11pm

17 New Zealand Lane, Duffield DE56 4BZ
Telephone: 01332 841156   www.okra.org.uk

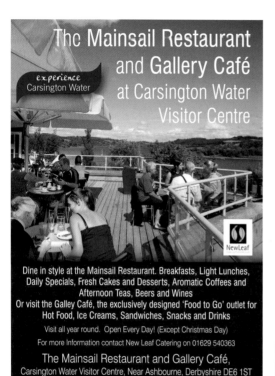

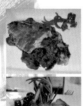

The Bulls Head Repton

www.thebullsheadrepton.co.uk

WOW – this place is stunning. It is a high quality pub with dining rooms offering fabulous food and drink.

You will love the interior. The pub is steeped in character with roaring fires, old beams and an original stone floor. With plenty of stylish touches, the atmosphere at the Bulls Head is a country pub dream.

It's all about informal quality, with superb food and drink in a relaxed place. The food is fresh – really fresh. You can tell that from the menus, which are changed and printed every day. The main menu is on offer lunchtime and evening every day, and a Sunday roast menu is available all day on Sundays.

In two years since opening, the pub has won several food awards and the highest scores possible for their real ales on the 'Cask Mark' judging criteria. It sells wonderful coffee, bottled beers served in frozen glasses, there are sixty-three different bottles of wine on the wine list, a magical outside terrace with the biggest umbrella in Europe. This is not an average pub. Just have a look at their fabulous website then, go and take a look at the real thing. You won't be disappointed.

Oh, by the way – they serve real chips made from real potatoes by a real person !

Directions: Just south of Derby,

Repton is 2 miles from the A50 / A38 junction (the Toyota junction). Look for the twinkle lights in the trees in the centre of Repton.

Opening Times: Noon until midnight every day. Food offered lunchtime and evenings every day (and all day on Sunday) The Bulls Head, 84 High Street, Repton, Derbyshire DE65 6GF 01283 70 44 22

THE
BULLS HEAD
R E P T O N
Pub and Dining Rooms

Best Derbyshire Pub
Winner

east midlands tourism
enjoy england
excellence
awards
2008

84 High Street • Repton • Derbyshire • DE65 6GF • Tel 01283 70 44 22
www.thebullsheadrepton.co.uk

Create...

the environment

food
just
tastes
better
in a
quality
kitchen

PRIDE OF PLACE
KITCHENS FOR INDIVIDUALS

Quality and Affordable Kitchens • Bathrooms • Bedrooms • Studies and Home Offices
www.pride-of-place.co.uk
Pride Of Place, 17 Nottingham Road, Alfreton, Derbyshire, DE55 7HL. Tel: 01773 836438

give taste as a gift
buy taste derbyshire &
nottinghamshire
online for only £3.50
and we will post it
FREE of charge*
visit our web site
www.tastederbyshire.co.uk

*UK only

Send cheque payable to
Images Publishing Limited

to Images Publishing Limited
Victoria House, Market Place
Crich, Matlock
Derbyshire DE4 5DD

or phone 01773 850050
(credit and debit cards taken)

or visit our website www.tastederbyshire.co.uk

taste directory:

Recipes:

Food and drink producers and suppliers:

Arrow Farm Shop
Steetley, Worksop
Nottinghamshire S80 3DZ
01909 723018
www.arrowfarmshop.co.uk

Chatsworth Farm Shop
Pilsley, Bakewell, Derbyshire
DE45 1UF
01246 583392
www.chatsworth.org

Colston Bassett Store
Church Gate, Colston Bassett
Nottinghamshire NG12 3FE
01949 81321
www.colstonbassettstore.com

Croots
Farnah House Farm, Wirksworth Road, Duffield,
Derbyshire DE56 4AQ
01332 843032
www.croots.co.uk

Denstone Hall Farm Shop & Café
Denstone, Staffordshire
ST14 5HS
01889 590050
www.denstonehall.co.uk

Fruit & Veg Mini-Mart
The Croft, Crich, Derbyshire
DE4 5DD

Gonalston Farm Shop
Southwell Road, Gonalston
Nottinghamshire NG14 7DR
01159 665666
www.gonalstonfarmshop.co.uk

Highfield House Farm Shop
B5057 Darley Road, Stonedge
Chesterfield S45 0LW
01246 590817 / 01246 591327
www.highfieldhousefarm.co.uk

Holloway Village Butchers
Lea Shaw Road, Holloway
Derbyshire DE4 5AT
01629 534333

Jerry Howarth Butchers
7 King Street, Belper
Derbyshire DE56 1PW
01773 822557

Oakfield Farm Shop
Oakfield Farm, Belper Road
Stanley Common DE7 6FP
0115 9305358
www.oakfieldfarm.co.uk

Olivers Organics
508 Duffield Road, Allestree
Derby DE22 2DL
01332 554890
www.oliversorganics.co.uk

Peak Ales
Barn Brewery, Cunnery Barn Chatsworth
01246 583737
www.peakales.co.uk

Peak District Dairy
Healthy Grange, Tideswell, Derbyshire
01298 871786
www.peakdistrictdairy.co.uk

Mr Pitchfork's Pickles
W39 Nottingham Business Centre
Lenton Boulevard
Nottingham NG7 2BY
01159 178037 / 07761428961

Superior Meats & Vegetables
38 High Street, Old Whittington
Chesterfield, S41 9JT
01246 450454

The Complete Cook Shop
Unit 3, Granby Croft, Matlock Street, Bakewell,
DE45 1EE
01629 814499
www.bake-well.co.uk

The Friendly Farmer
A17/A46/A1 Roundabout
Newark, Nottinghamshire
NG24 2NY
01636 612461

The Honey Pot
Markeaton Craft Village, Markeaton Lane, Derby
01332 203893
www.localhoney.co.uk

The National Forest Spring Water Company Ltd
Highfields, Cockshut Lane
Melbourne, Derbyshire
DE73 8DG
01332 862699
www.nationalforestspringwater.co.uk

The Pudding Room
Nr Carsington Water
Ashbourne, Derbyshire
DE6 1NQ
01629 540413
www.thepuddingroomderbyshire.co.uk

Trinity Farm Organics
Awsworth Lane
Cossall, Nottinghamshire
NG16 2RZ
0115 9442545
www.trinityfarmshop.co.uk

Redgate's Farm Shop
Coney Grey Farm
Mansfield Road, Brinsley
Nottinghamshire NG16 5AE
01773 713403

Redwood Smokehouse
Bolsover Business Park
Woodhouse Lane, Bolsover
01246 827972
www.jaquest.co.uk

Scaddows Farm Shop
Scaddows Farm, Ticknall
Derby DE73 7JP
01332 865709
www.scaddowsfarm.co.uk

Superior Meats & Vegetables
38 High Street,
Old Whittington,
Chesterfield,
Derbyshire
01246 450454

Wee Dram
5 Portland Square
Bakewell, Derbyshire
DE45 1HA
01629 812235
www.weedram.co.uk

Welbeck Farm Shop
Welbeck Estate
Worksop, Nottinghamshire
01909 478725
www.thewelbeckfarmshop.co.u

White Post Farm Shop
Farsnfield, Nottinghamshire
NG22 8HL
01623 883847
www.whitepostfarm.co.uk

Restaurants:

Archie's
The Barn, 4 Bridge Street
Sandiacre, Nottingham
NG10 5QT
01159 499324
www.archiesrestaurant.co.uk

Bay Tree Restaurant
4 Potter Street, Melbourne
Derbyshire DE73 1DW
01332 863358
www.baytreerestaurant.co.uk

Bourne's at Denby
Denby Visitor Centre
Derby Road (B6179)
Denby, Derbyshire
DE5 8NX
01773 740799
www.denbyvisitorcentre.co.uk

Chevin Coffee Shop
De Bradelei Stores
Chapel Street, Belper
Derbyshire DE56 1AR
01773 882442
www.debradelei.com

Mainsail Restaurant
Carsington Water
Ashbourne
Derbyshire
DE6 1ST
01629 540363

The Saracen's Head Hotel
Market Place, Southwell
Nottinghamshire, NG25 0HE
01636 812701

The Bull's Head
84 High Street, Repton
Derbyshire DE65 6GJ
01283 704422
www.thebullsheadrepton.co.uk

The Coach & Horses
Main Street, Thurgarton
Nottinghamshire NG14 7GY
01636 831311

The Denby Lodge
Church Street, Denby Village
Derbyshire DE5 8PH
01332 881089
www.denbylodge.co.uk

The Old Smithy
Chapel Hill, Beeley
Derbyshire DE4 2NR
01629 734666

The Saracen's Head Hotel
Market Place, Southwell
Nottinghamshire, NG25 0HE
01636 812701

The Old Bakery
Coffee Shop and Restaurant
Market Place, Cromford,
Derbyshire DE4 3RE

Iberico World Tapas Restaurant
The Shire Hall, High Pavement
Lace Market, Nottingham
NG1 1HN
01159 410410
www.ibericotapas.com

O-kra
17 New Zealand Lane
Duffield DE56 4BZ
01332 841156
www.okra.co.uk

Sanam Tandoori Restaurant
50 King Street, Alfreton
Derbyshire, DE55 7DD
01773 830690

World Service Restaurant/Lounge Bar
Newdigate House, Castle Gate
Nottingham NG1 6AF
01158 475587
www.worldservicerestaurant.com

Dining out reports:

Iberico World Tapas Restaurant
The Shire Hall, High Pavement
Lace Market, Nottingham
NG1 1HN
01159 410410
www.ibericotapas.com

The Saracen's Head Hotel
Market Place, Southwell
Nottinghamshire, NG25 0HE
01636 812701

Okra
17 New Zealand Lane
Duffield DE56 4BZ
01332 841156
www.okra.co.uk

Sanam Tandoori Restaurant
50 King Street, Alfreton
Derbyshire, DE55 7DD
01773 830690

The Old Bakery
Coffee Shop and Restaurant
Market Place, Cromford,
Derbyshire DE4 3RE

World Service Restaurant/Lounge Bar
Newdigate House, Castle Gate
Nottingham NG1 6AF
01158 475587

Kitchens and equipment:

The Denby Pottery Company Ltd.
Denby
Derbyshire
DE5 8NX
England
01773 740799
01773 740749
www.denby.co.uk

Kitchen Solutions Ltd
St Andrews Court
96 Station Road, Langley Mill Nottinghamshire
NG16 4BP
01773 716465
www.kitchen-solutions.net

Natural Stones Sales Ltd
Old Station Yard, Rowsley, Matlock DE4 2EJ
01629 735507
www.naturalstonesalesltd.co.uk

Pride of Place
Nottingham Road, Alfreton Derbyshire DE55 7HL
01773 836438
www.pride-of-place.co.uk

Solutions
121 Mansfield Road
Sutton in Ashfield
Nottinghamshire NG17 4FL
01623 515793
www.directplumbing.co.uk

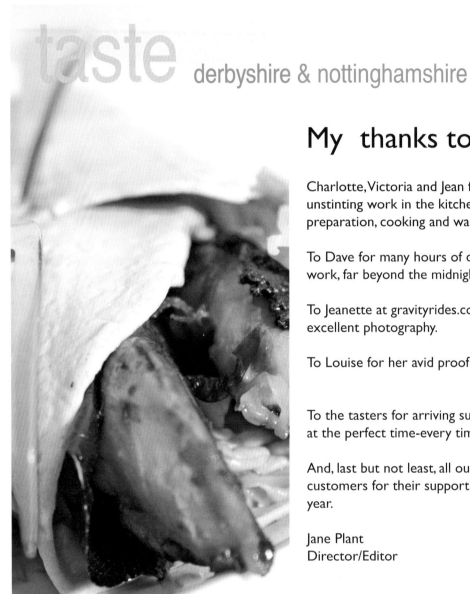

taste derbyshire & nottinghamshire

My thanks to:

Charlotte, Victoria and Jean for their unstinting work in the kitchen on food preparation, cooking and washing up.

To Dave for many hours of design work, far beyond the midnight hour!

To Jeanette at gravityrides.com for her excellent photography.

To Louise for her avid proofreading.

To the tasters for arriving suspiciously at the perfect time-every time.

And, last but not least, all our customers for their support again this year.

Jane Plant
Director/Editor

taste derbyshire is published by

IMAGES PUBLISHING LIMITED

Victoria House, Market Place, Crich DE4 5DD

Tel: 01773 850050 Fax: 01773 850058
www.tastederbyshire.co.uk

Publishers of
Country Images Magazine, County Golfer and taste derbyshire & nottinghamshire

Printed at Buxton Press

our thanks to:

The Denby Pottery Company Ltd
Denby
Derbyshire
DE5 8NX
Telephone: +44 (0)1773 740700
Fax: +44 (0)1773 570211
www.denby.co.uk

Farnah House Farm
Wirksworth Road, Duffield
DE56 4AQ
www.croots.co.uk

Gravity Rides
t: 07793 739684
www.gravityrides.co.uk
e: jen@gravityrides.co.uk

If you enjoy life you will love

COUNTRY
Images
magazine

Each month we feature recipes, farm shops, restaurant reviews, eating places and food competitions alongside articles of interest including, fashion, leisure, walks, motoring, gardening and much more.

Country Images is delivered FREE to 34,000 carefully selected homes every month in Derbyshire and Nottinghamshire.

Based in Crich, Derbyshire, we are a local company reflecting the community in which we live.

Let us promote your business

- We offer excellent customer service.
- Free professional advert design.
- Expert advice from our experienced sales executives who are happy to spend time at your business helping you with your promotional needs.

Putting *your* business in the spotlight

Call us now on
01773 850500

Images Publishing Limited
a local, family-owned company
serving the local community